The Way to Wealth
Workbook

This workbook helps you implement the ideas in these books by Brian Tracy from Entrepreneur Press

The Way to Wealth:
The Journey Begins: Success Strategies of Wealthy Entrepreneurs

The Way to Wealth in Action:
Building a Highly Profitable Business

The Way to Wealth
Workbook

Blueprints for Success

Brian Tracy

EP
Entrepreneur Press

Publisher: Jere Calmes
Cover Design: Beth Hansen-Winter
Production and Editorial Services: CWL Publishing Enterprises, Inc., Madison, Wisconsin, www.cwlpub.com

© 2008 by Entrepreneur Media, Inc. and Brian Tracy

All rights reserved.
Reproduction of any part of this work beyond that permitted by Section 107 or 108 of the 1976 United States Copyright Act without the express permission of the copyright owner is unlawful. Requests for permission or further information should be addressed to the Business Products Division, Entrepreneur Media, Inc.

This publication is designed to provide accurate and authoritative information in regard to the subject matter covered. It is sold with the understanding that the publisher is not engaged in rendering legal, accounting, or other professional services. If legal advice or other expert assistance is required, the services of a competent professional person should be sought.
—From a Declaration of Principles jointly adopted by a Committee of the American Bar Association and a Committee of Publishers and Associations

ISBN   13: 978-1-599181-52-3
       10: 1-533181-52-5

Library of Congress Cataloging-in-Publication Data available.

Printed in Canada.

11 10 09 08 07   10 9 8 7 6 5 3 2 1

Use these tabs to navigate this Workbook

Business Blueprints — **Chapter 1**

Strategy Blueprints — **Chapter 2**

Marketing Blueprints — **Chapter 3**

Sales Blueprints — **Chapter 4**

Financial Blueprints — **Chapter 5**

Personal Blueprints — **Chapter 6**

Productivity and Performance Blueprints — **Chapter 7**

CONTENTS

Introduction	**xi**
1. Business Blueprints	**1**
1. Business Strategic Planning Questionnaire	2
2. Business Assessment—Reasons for Success and Failure	13
3. Management Skills Assessment	24
4. Seven Key Result Areas in Business	28
5. Seven Responsibilities of Leadership	31
6. How to Hire—Guidelines	33
7. Hiring the Best People	35
8. How to Build a Top Team	37
9. How to Fire	41
10. Making the Firing Decision	42
11. Seven Qualities of Leadership	44
12. Seven Keys to Project Management	46
13. Seven Questions for Any Investment	47
2. Strategic Blueprints	**49**
1. Strategic Planning Questions	50
2. Business Planning Process	52
3. Ten Keys to Business Success	58
4. Seven Ways to Build an Entrepreneurial Business Faster	61
5. Your Core Business	63
6. The Driving Force in Strategy	65
7. Opportunity Analysis	67
8. Seven Steps to Business Profitability	69
9. Choosing the Right Location	71
10. Money and Financial Goals	79

Contents

 11. Seven Steps to Problem Solving   80
 12. Twelve Critical Orientations for Business and Personal Success   82
 13. Time Allocation Exercise   85

3. Marketing Blueprints   89
 1. Seven Keys to Marketing Success   91
 2. Seven Questions for Market Planning   93
 3. Four Principles of Marketing Strategy   95
 4. Seven P's of the Marketing Mix   101
 5. Finding a New Product or Service   104
 6. How to Do Fast, Cheap Market Research   107
 7. Nine Great Marketing Questions   109
 8. Seven Reasons Why People Buy Things   112
 9. Key Concerns in Making a Buying Decision   114
 10. Becoming the Quality Choice   116
 11. Buying Customers—Determining Your Costs of Acquisition   120
 12. Lifetime Value of a Customer   121
 13. How to Write Effective Advertising   122
 14. 24 Ways to Sell Your Product or Service   125

4. Sales Blueprints   127
 1. Sales Skills Assessment   138
 2. Sales Planning Process   142
 3. Seven Ways of Selling   145
 4. Seven Qualities of Top Salespeople   150
 5. Seven Best Sales-Closing Techniques   151
 6. Four Levels of Customer Service   152
 7. Seven Keys to Effective Networking   154
 8. Seven Questions to Set Priorities in Selling   155

5. Financial Blueprints   157
 1. Critical Success Factors, Benchmarks, and Metrics   159
 2. 23 Ways to Get the Money You Need   161
 3. Borrowing from Your Bank   169
 4. Profit Analysis and Maximization   172
 5. Double Your Income Seven Ways   174
 6. Double Your Income—Exercises   176
 7. Fifteen Profit-Making Strategies   178
 8. Determining Your Costs   185
 9. Conduct a Breakeven Analysis   188
 10. Twelve Ways to Set Your Prices   189
 11. The Seven Systems You Need   196
 12. Seven Keys to Legal Agreements   200
 13. Rules Learned from Lawsuits and Arbitration   201

Contents

6. Personal Blueprints — 203
1. The Seven Mental Laws of Success — 204
2. Personal Analysis — 207
3. Seven Qualities of Self-Made Millionaires — 216
4. Personal Effectiveness Assessment — 217
5. List of Values — 219
6. Achieving Clarity with Your Goals — 221
7. Seven Questions for Goal Setting — 223
8. Major Definite Purpose — 225
9. Seven Key Concepts for Success — 226
10. Seven Truths About You — 229

7. Productivity and Performance Blueprints — 231
1. Seven Disciplines for Success — 232
2. Seven Steps to Better Time Management — 233
3. Seven Steps to Productivity Improvement — 234
4. Highest-Value Activities — 235
5. Seven Secrets of Superb Health — 238
6. The 1000% Formula — 240
7. Seven Steps to Mental Fitness — 242
8. Seven Keys to Achieving Balance in Life — 243
9. The Seven C's of Effectiveness — 245
10. Double Your Time Off — 247
11. Simplification — 249
12. Simplification Exercise — 250
13. Decision Making — 252
14. Seven Rules for the 21st Century — 253
15. Daily Affirmations — 254

About the Author — 255

Brian Tracy University of Sales and Entrepreneurship — 256

Business Coaching Opportunity — 257

Brian Tracy—Speaker, Author, Consultant — 258

INTRODUCTION

Welcome to Blueprints for Business Success!

The primary difference between successful business owners and those who struggle most of the time is their ability **to think**.

In the pages ahead, you will learn a series of essential ideas and blueprints that you must know to survive and thrive in a competitive business. Throughout this book, you will be required to ask and answer a series of questions about yourself and your business operations. These key questions will help you to think, plan, decide, and take better actions to achieve your goals for sales, profitability, and business growth.

Your answers to these **key questions** will give you insights into your strengths and weaknesses—business and personal—and help you to achieve better balance between your work and personal life.

These questions and checklists will help you whether you are already in business or you are thinking about starting a business. They can make all the difference between success and failure.

You can return to these tools and blueprints again and again and review them with your business partners, staff, and family. Each time you analyze your business with them, you will gain additional insights. These insights will enable you to make better decisions and get better results than ever before.

CHAPTER ONE

Business Blueprints

In this chapter:

1.	Business Strategic Planning Questionnaire	2
2	Business Assessment—Reasons for Success and Failure	13
3.	Management Skills Assessment	24
4.	Seven Key Result Areas in Business	28
5.	Seven Responsibilities of Leadership	31
6.	How to Hire—Guidelines	33
7.	Hiring the Best People	35
8.	How to Build a Top Team	37
9.	How to Fire	41
10.	Making the Firing Decision	42
11.	Seven Qualities of Leadership	44
12.	Seven Keys to Project Management	46
13.	Seven Questions for Any Investment	47

WAY TO WEALTH WORKBOOK: BLUEPRINTS FOR BUSINESS SUCCESS

1. Business Strategic Planning Questionnaire

Your ability to think, plan, and act strategically will affect your sales and profitability more than anything else you do. Very often, a single change in your activities can lead to a major difference in your results.

If you do not know the answers to these questions, or if you have the wrong answers, you can make mistakes in marketing, sales, and business operations that can be fatal to your business.

Answer each question the best you can. If you do not know the answer or if you are unsure, it is important that you find out as soon as possible.

1. What business are you in? Define your business in terms of what you actually **do** for your customers to improve their life or work.

    1. _____

    2. _____

    3. _____

2. What is the **mission** of your company? Define your mission in terms of what you want to achieve, avoid, or preserve for your customers.

    1. _____

    2. _____

    3. _____

3. How do you want your customers to talk about your company, think about your company, or **describe** your company to others? What **words** do you want them to use?

    1. _____

    2. _____

    3. _____

4. Who is your **perfect customer**? Describe him or her in terms of age, income, education, occupation, location, and whatever other factors are appropriate for your industry.

    1. Age? _____

    2. Income? _____

    3. Occupation? _____

Chapter 1. Business Blueprints

    4. Education? _____

    5. Need or problem? _____

    6. Other? _____

5. What does your ideal customer consider **value**? What benefits does your customer seek or expect in dealing with you?

    1. _____

    2. _____

    3. _____

6. What are your company's **core competencies**? What special skills or abilities does your company possess that enable you to fulfill the needs of your customers?

    1. _____

    2. _____

    3. _____

7. What does your company do extremely well? In what areas do you perform in an exceptional fashion? What makes you **superior** to your competitors?

    1. _____

    2. _____

    3. _____

8. Who are your **competitors**? Who else sells your same product or service to your prospective customers?

    1. _____

    2. _____

    3. _____

9. Who are your **biggest** or main competitors?

    1. _____

    2. _____

    3. _____

Way to Wealth Workbook: Blueprints for Business Success

10. Who are your **secondary** competitors? Who offers an alternative to what you sell?

    1. _____
    2. _____
    3. _____

11. **Why** do your customers buy from your competitors? What benefits do they receive from your competitors that they don't receive from you?

    1. _____
    2. _____
    3. _____

12. Which of your products or services give you your **highest profit**? Where do you get your highest payoff? What do you do that gives you your highest return on effort or investment?

    1. _____
    2. _____
    3. _____

13. Which products, services, markets, customers, or activities should your company **abandon, eliminate, or leave** to free up more time for higher-value, more profitable activities?

    1. _____
    2. _____
    3. _____

14. What could you do to **attract** your competitors' customers and get them to buy from you?

    1. _____
    2. _____
    3. _____

Chapter 1. Business Blueprints

15. How could you improve your marketing methods to **generate more leads** and attract more potential customers?

    1. _____
    2. _____
    3. _____

16. What is your company's area of **specialization**? What are your products or services uniquely suited to do and for whom?

    1. _____
    2. _____
    3. _____

17. What is your area of **differentiation** or excellence? In what ways are you superior to your competitors?

    1. _____
    2. _____
    3. _____

18. What is your specific **competitive advantage**? What qualities of your products, services, or business make you better than 90% of businesses in your industry?

    1. _____
    2. _____
    3. _____

19. What **type of customers** can benefit the most from the superior benefits of your products or services?

    1. _____
    2. _____
    3. _____

Way to Wealth Workbook: Blueprints for Business Success

20. In what areas of advertising, promotion, and selling should you **concentrate your energy** and resources to maximize your sales and profits?

    1. _____

    2. _____

    3. _____

21. How could you **convert** more of your prospects into paying customers? What methods of sale could you use?

    1. _____

    2. _____

    3. _____

22. Which customers should you **phase out or abandon** because they are no longer worth the time and energy they take to satisfy?

    1. _____

    2. _____

    3. _____

23. What **activities** should you abandon or de-emphasize so you can have more time for those activities that offer the highest possible return on your investment of time and energy?

    1. _____

    2. _____

    3. _____

24. What is your current **positioning** in your marketplace? How do people think and talk about you and your business when you are not there? What **words** do they use to describe you?

    1. _____

    2. _____

    3. _____

Chapter 1. Business Blueprints

25. What is your **brand** in your market today? What are you known for in your market? If you don't have a brand in your market, what would you like to be known for to your customers?

    1. _____
    2. _____
    3. _____

26. What **should** your brand be? What words or description would you like to own in your customers' minds? What kind of a reputation would be most helpful for you to develop?

    1. _____
    2. _____
    3. _____

27. What could you **change or improve** about your products, services, or business to begin creating a more favorable brand image in your customers' minds?

    1. _____
    2. _____
    3. _____

28. What are your three greatest weaknesses as an organization?

    1. _____
    2. _____
    3. _____

29. What are your three biggest **obstacles** to achieving higher levels of sales and profitability?

    1. _____
    2. _____
    3. _____

Way to Wealth Workbook: Blueprints for Business Success

30. What are the three greatest potential **threats** to your business today? What are the **worst things** that could go wrong?

    1. _____

    2. _____

    3. _____

31. Looking into the **future**, what are three worst things that could happen to hurt your business one year from today?

    1. _____

    2. _____

    3. _____

32. What three steps could you take immediately to **guard against** these possible dangers?

    1. _____

    2. _____

    3. _____

33. What are your three areas of **greatest opportunity** for the future, based on the trends in your business?

    1. _____

    2. _____

    3. _____

34. What three steps could you take immediately to **take advantage of** these opportunities?

    1. _____

    2. _____

    3. _____

Chapter 1. Business Blueprints

35. What three **core competencies** or skills should you begin developing today to ensure that you will be ready for the opportunities of tomorrow?

   1. _____
   2. _____
   3. _____

36. How is **technology** affecting your business? What changes does the Internet cause in the way you do business?

   1. _____
   2. _____
   3. _____

37. What are you doing today that you would not get into again if you had to do it over—**knowing what you know now**?

   1. _____
   2. _____
   3. _____

38. **Reorganization:** What changes should you make in your business, with regard to people and expenses, to improve both effectiveness and efficiency?

   1. _____
   2. _____
   3. _____

39. **Restructuring:** How could you shift more of your time and resources into the top 20% of activities that account for 80% of your profits?

   1. _____
   2. _____
   3. _____

Way to Wealth Workbook: Blueprints for Business Success

40. **Reinventing:** Imagine your business burned to the ground today. What products, services, and activities would you start up again immediately?

   1. _____
   2. _____
   3. _____

   What products, services, or activities would you **not start up** again today?

   1. _____
   2. _____
   3. _____

41. **Reengineering:** Analyze every step of your business activities. What could you **simplify**, **outsource**, **eliminate**, or **discontinue**?

   1. _____
   2. _____
   3. _____

42. What could you do to simplify any business process by **reducing** the number of steps in the process?

   1. _____
   2. _____
   3. _____

43. What activities could you **eliminate** completely to speed up the process of producing your products and services?

   1. _____
   2. _____
   3. _____

Chapter 1. Business Blueprints

44. What activities could you **outsource** to other individuals or companies to free yourself to sell and deliver more of your products and services?

   1. _____
   2. _____
   3. _____

45. What activities could you **discontinue** with no significant loss of sales or revenue?

   1. _____
   2. _____
   3. _____

46. Is there any **person** in your business life—a customer, employee, associate—whom you wouldn't acquire, hire, or get involved with today, knowing what you know now?

   1. _____
   2. _____
   3. _____

47. If you could start your business or career over again today, what would you do **differently**?

   1. _____
   2. _____
   3. _____

48. What skills, abilities, and talents do you have that have been most responsible for your **successes** to date?

   1. _____
   2. _____
   3. _____

Way to Wealth Workbook: Blueprints for Business Success

49. If you could be absolutely **excellent** in any one area, which one area would most help you achieve your goals?

   1. _____

   2. _____

   3. _____

50. What **one action** are you going to take immediately as a result of your answers to the above questions?

   _____
   _____
   _____

Notes

Chapter 1. Business Blueprints

2. Business Assessment—Reasons for Success and Failure

There are specific reasons for business success and for business failure. The greater clarity you have regarding these measures in your business, the better decisions and actions you will be able to make and take. By analyzing and comparing your business against the reasons for success and failure, you will gain key insights necessary to improve your sales and profitability.

You've heard it said, "What you don't know can't hurt you." Well, in business, the opposite is true: "What you don't know can cause you to fail."

To get the most out of this analysis, follow these steps:

1. Read each reason for business success or failure and give yourself a grade of 1–10, worst to best, in each area.
2. Collect your answers on the chart at the end to get a snapshot of your business today.
3. Identify your strongest and weakest areas.
    - You should be above a 7 on the reasons for business success.
    - You should be below a 3 on the reasons for business failure.
4. Complete the exercises at the end and answer the seven questions.
5. Make a commitment to take at least one action immediately.

If this exercise is helpful to you, you may want to enroll in "Increase Your Profits!" or "Start Your Own Business!" at Brian Tracy University—**www.briantracyu.com**—to learn the essential skills you need to achieve business success.

Take action each day to increase your likelihood of success and reduce your potential for failure. You will be on your way to financial independence.

Ten Reasons for Business Success

Give yourself a grade of 1–10 in each area.

1. Your **product** or **service** is ***well suited*** to the needs of the current market.
    a) You are selling, delivering, and getting paid for your product or service.
    b) You are earning a comfortable profit on sales.
    c) Your customers are happy.

Grade:	1	2	3	4	5	6	7	8	9	10

2. You developed a **complete business plan** before you began operations.
    a) You have analyzed your business and your market and you have a complete plan for sales, marketing, and business operations.

13

b) You have planned out every detail of your business and you work your plan each day.

| Grade: | 1 | 2 | 3 | 4 | 5 | 6 | 7 | 8 | 9 | 10 |

3. You have done a **complete market analysis** of your product and its most attractive features.

   a) You have determined your *competitive advantage* in your market and are prepared to exploit it.
   b) You have a complete advertising, marketing, and promotion plan for your products or services.
   c) You have a complete sales methodology and process to achieve the sales targets you have set.

| Grade: | 1 | 2 | 3 | 4 | 5 | 6 | 7 | 8 | 9 | 10 |

4. You have created a system for bookkeeping, accounting, and **complete financial control**.

   a) You have a budget for each business activity.
   b) You continually measure your results against your projections.
   c) You move quickly whenever there is a variance from your projections.

| Grade: | 1 | 2 | 3 | 4 | 5 | 6 | 7 | 8 | 9 | 10 |

5. Your **key people** show a high degree of **competence, capability**, and **integrity**.

   a) You have clear job and responsibility descriptions for each function.
   b) You have carefully selected and placed competent people in each important job.
   c) There is no one in your business whom you would not hire again today if you had it to do over.

| Grade: | 1 | 2 | 3 | 4 | 5 | 6 | 7 | 8 | 9 | 10 |

6. You are **well organized**, manage your time well, and have measures of performance for each key job.

   a) You always work on your most important tasks.
   b) Everyone knows exactly what results are expected of him or her and how he or she will be measured and rewarded.
   c) You regularly review key result areas and standards of performance for each person.

| Grade: | 1 | 2 | 3 | 4 | 5 | 6 | 7 | 8 | 9 | 10 |

Chapter 1. Business Blueprints

7. You are **clear**, **determined**, and **persistent** in your desire to succeed and profit.
   a) You have clear goals for yourself and your business in every area.
   b) You focus on solutions rather than problems.
   c) For you, "Failure is not an option!"

   | **Grade:** | 1 | 2 | 3 | 4 | 5 | 6 | 7 | 8 | 9 | 10 |

8. You **communicate clearly** and **effectively** with all the key people in your business.
   a) Everyone knows your business goals and how he or she is involved in achieving them.
   b) You have regular information-sharing meetings with your staff; there are no secrets.
   c) You keep your bankers and your partners regularly informed about developments in the business.

   | **Grade:** | 1 | 2 | 3 | 4 | 5 | 6 | 7 | 8 | 9 | 10 |

9. There is **strong** momentum in **sales** and a continual emphasis on **marketing**.
   a) You follow a written marketing plan that generates a steady stream of qualified leads.
   b) You have specific sales targets that you are committed to hitting—daily, weekly, monthly.
   c) You have a successful sales process that turns prospects into customers most of the time.

   | **Grade:** | 1 | 2 | 3 | 4 | 5 | 6 | 7 | 8 | 9 | 10 |

10. Everyone in your company thinks continually about acquiring, satisfying, and keeping customers. There is a continual **focus on customer acquisition**.
    a) The purpose of a business is to create and keep customers; all profits come from that.
    b) Customer satisfaction is the only measure of business success in the long term.
    c) If you are succeeding in this area, your customers are so happy with you that they recommend you to their friends.

    | **Grade:** | 1 | 2 | 3 | 4 | 5 | 6 | 7 | 8 | 9 | 10 |

Conclusion

The more you practice the ten reasons for business success, the greater will be your sales and profitability.

Reasons for Business Success

Area	Score
1. Product Fit	
2. Business Plan	
3. Market Analysis	
4. Complete Financial Control	
5. Key People	
6. Organization	
7. Determination/Persistence	
8. Communication	
9. Sales and Marketing	
10. Focus on Customer Acquisition	
Total Score	

Score:

    91–100 = Excellent

    81–90 = Above Average

    71–80 = Good

    60–70 = Average

    Below 60 = Below Average

Now divide your score by 10. Your business should average 7 or higher. *One key weakness* can be enough to put you out of business.

What **one action** are you going to take immediately as the result of your analysis above?

_____

_____

_____

Chapter 1. Business Blueprints

Fifteen Reasons for Business Failure

There are many common reasons for business failure. Every business owner is weak in one or more of these areas. Give yourself a grade of 1–10 in each area. How much is this reason a problem for you? Ask your staff and spouse (if you're married) to grade your company as well.

1. **Lack of Direction:** You have no goals, plans, or blueprints for action. As a result, everyone in the business is reacting to daily pressures, focused on operating rather than managing.

    a) The business does not have a written business plan, thought out in detail before beginning business operations. Without a clear, written plan, you are like a carpenter attempting to build a house without a blueprint.

    b) The business owner has not decided on his or her business values, vision, mission, and purpose. As a result, the business lurches from one problem or crisis to the next, like a drunk going from lamppost to lamppost.

    c) The business owner does not have clear, written goals and plans to guide him or her in the areas of business, money, family, and health. Without written goals and plans, you are like a person traveling in an unfamiliar land with no road signs or road maps.

Grade:	1	2	3	4	5	6	7	8	9	10

2. **Impatience:** The entrepreneur is unrealistic about how long it takes to achieve business results.

    a) Everything takes at least three times as long as you calculated.
    b) Everything costs at least twice as much as you thought it would.
    c) Nothing works properly the first time or the first few times.

Grade:	1	2	3	4	5	6	7	8	9	10

3. **Greed:** The entrepreneur thinks he or she can make a lot of money quickly and easily.

    a) Many businesses fail because the owner is looking for a way to make a quick killing and become an instant millionaire.
    b) "The only thing easy about money is losing it." (John D. Rockefeller)
    c) "Making money is like digging with a pin; losing money is like pouring water on the sand." (Japanese proverb)

Grade:	1	2	3	4	5	6	7	8	9	10

WAY TO WEALTH WORKBOOK: BLUEPRINTS FOR BUSINESS SUCCESS

4. **Action Without Thinking:** This is the cause of every failure.
   a) Inexperienced entrepreneurs often commit time and money foolishly, without considering the consequences.
   b) Acting impetuously, without taking the time to get the facts and think it through, can cost you a fortune in time and money.
   c) "No matter how far you have gone on the wrong road, turn back." (Turkish proverb)

   | Grade: | 1 | 2 | 3 | 4 | 5 | 6 | 7 | 8 | 9 | 10 |

5. **Poor Cost Control:** Many entrepreneurs spend too much money on unnecessary things, especially at the beginning.
   a) Resolve to conserve cash at all times, in every situation.
   b) Never buy if you can rent, never rent if you can borrow, and never do it in-house if some other company can do it for you.
   c) Practice frugality, frugality, frugality in all things.

   | Grade: | 1 | 2 | 3 | 4 | 5 | 6 | 7 | 8 | 9 | 10 |

6. **Poor Quality of Product/Service:** What you are offering is not excellent, better in some way than what your competitors are offering.
   a) You must be better, faster, and cheaper in at least three ways to break into a competitive market.
   b) You need a "unique selling proposition," a value that only you can offer your customers.

   | Grade: | 1 | 2 | 3 | 4 | 5 | 6 | 7 | 8 | 9 | 10 |

7. **Insufficient Working Capital:** The business owner was too optimistic and impatient.
   a) Accept that it takes a long time to get started and begin generating cash from sales.
   b) You need six months of cash reserves before starting your business.

   | Grade: | 1 | 2 | 3 | 4 | 5 | 6 | 7 | 8 | 9 | 10 |

8. **Bad or No Business Budgets:** Many business owners are flying by the seat of their pants. They do not know their exact financial situation.
   a) You need complete budgets, with every expense itemized, plus a 20% "fudge factor," to run your business.

Chapter 1. Business Blueprints

    b) Take the time to get accurate costs and expenses for every activity of your business.

| Grade: | 1 | 2 | 3 | 4 | 5 | 6 | 7 | 8 | 9 | 10 |

9. **Inadequate Financial Records:** The business owner either does not know how to maintain them or is too busy.

    a) You must know exactly how much money you have, how much you owe, how much is owed to you, and the deadlines for receipt or payment of all amounts.

    b) Set up a complete bookkeeping/accounting system so you always know where the money is and where it is going.

| Grade: | 1 | 2 | 3 | 4 | 5 | 6 | 7 | 8 | 9 | 10 |

10. **Loss of Momentum in the Sales Department:** The number-one reason for business failure is low sales.

    a) A drop in sales reduces cash flow and can lead to the collapse of the business.

    b) Get everyone in your company thinking about sales and customers all the time. Make sales the top priority of one or more people who are good at selling.

| Grade: | 1 | 2 | 3 | 4 | 5 | 6 | 7 | 8 | 9 | 10 |

11. **Failure to Anticipate Market Trends:** Products and services today have shorter and shorter life spans.

    a) Look ahead one, two, three years. Where is the market going? What are the trends?

    b) What products are you offering today that you wouldn't introduce again today, if you could start over?

    c) What changes are taking place in customer wants, needs, desires, and preferences?

| Grade: | 1 | 2 | 3 | 4 | 5 | 6 | 7 | 8 | 9 | 10 |

12. **Lack of Managerial/Business Ability or Experience:** Fully 90% of companies started by people with no business experience go broke within two years.

    a) Learn about and study every detail of the business, including customers, competitors, sales, costs, finances, and accounting.

    b) Read, listen, and attend seminars. Commit to continuous learning in your field.

| Grade: | 1 | 2 | 3 | 4 | 5 | 6 | 7 | 8 | 9 | 10 |

13. **Indecisiveness:** Success in business in a fast-moving, competitive market requires quick decisions.
    a) Because of the fear of failure, some people are paralyzed in the face of difficulties and setbacks.
    b) Because of the fear of rejection, many people avoid confronting others; companies often go broke because they keep a poor performer in a key position.

    | Grade: | 1 | 2 | 3 | 4 | 5 | 6 | 7 | 8 | 9 | 10 |

14. **Bad Human Relations:** The inability to get along well with others inside or outside your business can cause failure.
    a) Negative, hostile, angry people are often critical, complaining, and unkind to staff, suppliers, and even customers.
    b) "A man without a smile should never open a shop." (Chinese proverb)

    | Grade: | 1 | 2 | 3 | 4 | 5 | 6 | 7 | 8 | 9 | 10 |

15. **Diffusion of Effort:** Because of poor planning, the business owner is constantly reacting, eventually becoming overwhelmed with too much to do.
    a) The owner and every other person must have clear priorities in each area of the job.
    b) Keep asking, "What is the most important use of my time right now?"
    c) Ask, "What can I, and only I, do that, if I do it well, will make a real difference?"

    | Grade: | 1 | 2 | 3 | 4 | 5 | 6 | 7 | 8 | 9 | 10 |

Conclusion

The solution to common business problems is usually to do the opposite of what you did or did not do to cause the problem. Make a decision today to take action in at least one area, preferably the area that can help you the most to increase your profitability today.

Chapter 1. Business Blueprints

Reasons for Business Failure

Area	Score
1. Lack of Direction	
2. Impatience	
3. Greed	
4. Action Without Thinking	
5. Poor Cost Control	
6. Poor Quality of Product/Service	
7. Insufficient Working Capital	
8. Bad or No Business Budgets	
9. Inadequate Financial Records	
10. Loss of Sales Momentum	
11. Failure to Anticipate Market Trends	
12. Managerial Experience	
13. Indecisiveness	
14. Bad Human Relations	
15. Diffusion of Effort	
Total Score	

Now divide your total score by 15. An average score above **3** is a danger area that can sink your business. What is your plan to lower your score? Complete your answers to these seven questions.

Action Exercises

1. List three reasons why your business is **underperforming**.

    1. _____

    2. _____

    3. _____

WAY TO WEALTH WORKBOOK: BLUEPRINTS FOR BUSINESS SUCCESS

2. List three things you could do immediately to **improve results** in your business.

   1. _____
   2. _____
   3. _____

3. List three areas where you could **reduce** costs or expenses without hurting your business.

   1. _____
   2. _____
   3. _____

4. List three things—products, services, activities, or people—that you would **not** **introduce**, **start**, or **hire** again today, if you had it to do over.

   1. _____
   2. _____
   3. _____

5. List three reasons why your customers should **buy from you** rather than from your competitors.

   1. _____
   2. _____
   3. _____

6. List three actions you could take immediately to **improve your sales and marketing**.

   1. _____
   2. _____
   3. _____

Chapter 1. Business Blueprints

7. List three **key skill** areas where you would like to improve to make your business more successful.

   1. _____

   2. _____

   3. _____

What **one action** are you going to take immediately as the result of your answers to the above questions?

_____

_____

_____

Notes

Way to Wealth Workbook: Blueprints for Business Success

3. Management Skills Assessment

Why are some managers *more* efficient and effective than others?

Why do some managers build greater teams, departments, and companies and produce more outstanding results than others?

The difference between top managers and executives and average managers is almost always *knowledge* and *skill*.

Fortunately, all managerial skills are *learnable*. No one is born with them. Now we know what skills you need to achieve the best results in your job.

You may be just *one skill away* from dramatically improving your effectiveness. This Managerial Skills Assessment shows your strengths and weaknesses and where you have to work to maximize your potential.

Give yourself a grade of 1–10 for each of the following areas of key managerial skills. Be honest! Imagine you will be explaining your grade to others. The most important part of this Managerial Skills Assessment is that it shows you your strengths and weaknesses, and where you have to work to maximize your potential. Excellent performance in management is possible only if you are competent in the following areas:

1. **Planning:** You are competent and skilled in preparing detailed written plans of action for each of your areas of responsibility.
    a) You "think on paper" and rewrite your business goals until your plans are clear and easily understood.
    b) The people around you are clear about your plans and their roles in executing them.

    | Grade: | 1 | 2 | 3 | 4 | 5 | 6 | 7 | 8 | 9 | 10 |

2. **Organizing:** You are skilled and efficient at bringing together the people, money, resources, and facilities you need to carry out your plans.
    a) You organize everything you need in advance.
    b) Each person around you knows what you are trying to do and how you are trying to do it.

    | Grade: | 1 | 2 | 3 | 4 | 5 | 6 | 7 | 8 | 9 | 10 |

3. **Staffing/Recruiting:** You have developed the ability to select the right people to carry out your plans and get the job done.
    a) You have a tested, proven interview process that you use in finding the right people.

Chapter 1. Business Blueprints

    b) You have a proven selection process that ensures that you choose the right people most of the time.

Grade:	1	2	3	4	5	6	7	8	9	10

4. **Delegating:** You know how to delegate the task to the right person in the right way.
   a) You delegate important tasks to people of proven competence.
   b) You delegate tasks in such a way that the other person knows exactly what you want, when and how you want it, and how it is to be achieved.

Grade:	1	2	3	4	5	6	7	8	9	10

5. **Supervising:** You are capable of ensuring that the job is done on time and to required standards.
   a) You set up a regular reporting schedule and inspect what you expect.
   b) You allow maximum freedom of action with clear expectations and areas of control.

Grade:	1	2	3	4	5	6	7	8	9	10

6. **Measuring:** You establish clear measures and standards for each key job and activity.
   a) You know the key result measures required of you by your boss, customers, and superiors.
   b) Everyone who reports to you knows exactly what he or she is expected to do, in what order of priority, and how successful performance will be measured and rewarded.

Grade:	1	2	3	4	5	6	7	8	9	10

7. **Reporting:** You have established methods to report your results to the key people to whom you are responsible.
   a) You provide adequate, accurate, and timely reports on results and activities to your boss and others who require them.
   b) You ensure that your reports are prepared and presented in such a way that they are understood and accepted.

Grade:	1	2	3	4	5	6	7	8	9	10

8. **Productivity:** You are constantly seeking new, better, and faster methods and techniques to do the job more efficiently.
   a) You continually reorganize, restructure, and reengineer to reduce costs, complexity, and delays.
   b) You continually set better priorities and concentrate your people and resources on more valuable tasks and activities.

   | **Grade:** | 1 | 2 | 3 | 4 | 5 | 6 | 7 | 8 | 9 | 10 |

9. **Innovation:** You continually seek out new ways to increase sales, cut costs, and improve productivity.
   a) You keep current with new technology and look for ways to use it to get the job done faster, better, and cheaper.
   b) You encourage a creative climate, rewarding ideas for innovate approaches and solutions.

   | **Grade:** | 1 | 2 | 3 | 4 | 5 | 6 | 7 | 8 | 9 | 10 |

10. **Profitability:** You are constantly looking for ways to make the organization more profitable.
    a) You are always looking for ways to increase sales from new or existing products, boost cash flow, and improve net profits.
    b) You continually seek out and practice ways to cut costs and expenditures.

    | **Grade:** | 1 | 2 | 3 | 4 | 5 | 6 | 7 | 8 | 9 | 10 |

Chapter 1. Business Blueprints

Managerial Skills Assessment

Area	Score
1. Planning	
2. Organizing	
3. Staffing/Recruiting	
4. Delegating	
5. Supervising	
6. Measuring	
7. Reporting	
8. Productivity	
9. Innovation	
10. Profitability	
Total Score	

Add all numbers and evaluate your score.

Score: 91–100 = Excellent
81–90 = Above Average
71–80 = Good
60–70 = Average
Below 60 = Below Average

"Managers are made, not born. There may be naturally born managers, but there are so few of them that they make no difference in the great scheme of things."
—Peter Drucker

The fact is that you must be proficient in a wide range of managerial skills if you want to be the best, if you want to fulfill your potential for managerial effectiveness.

Key Point: A weakness in one important skill area can be enough to hold you back or undermine your effectiveness in many other areas.

All managerial skills are learnable. You can learn any skill you need to become excellent in managing and getting results through others.

WAY TO WEALTH WORKBOOK: BLUEPRINTS FOR BUSINESS SUCCESS

4. Seven Key Result Areas in Business

There are seven areas of business operations where you must absolutely, positively achieve results if your business is to survive and thrive. A weakness in any one of these areas can lead to underperformance of your business and even failure.

Give yourself a grade of 1-10 in each area. Then decide on three steps you could take to improve.

1. **Productivity:** Your business is operated efficiently and you achieve excellent returns on the amount of money and time invested in every business activity.

   | **Grade:** | 1 | 2 | 3 | 4 | 5 | 6 | 7 | 8 | 9 | 10 |

   What three steps could you take immediately to increase output and results while reducing costs and expenses?

   1. _____
   2. _____
   3. _____

2. **Customer Satisfaction:** Your customers are so happy with the products and services you sell and the way you treat them that they buy over and over again and tell their friends.

   | **Grade:** | 1 | 2 | 3 | 4 | 5 | 6 | 7 | 8 | 9 | 10 |

   What three steps could you take immediately to increase customer satisfaction?

   1. _____
   2. _____
   3. _____

3. **Profitability and Cost Control:** You are continually seeking ways to increase profits and reduce costs in each area of your business.

   | **Grade:** | 1 | 2 | 3 | 4 | 5 | 6 | 7 | 8 | 9 | 10 |

Chapter 1. Business Blueprints

What three actions could you take immediately to increase your profits?

1. _____
2. _____
3. _____

4. **Quality:** Your products and services are consistently of excellent quality relative to your competitors' and you are committed to continuous and never-ending improvement.

| Grade: | 1 | 2 | 3 | 4 | 5 | 6 | 7 | 8 | 9 | 10 |

What three things could you do on a daily basis to ensure high and consistent levels of quality in your business?

1. _____
2. _____
3. _____

5. **People Building:** You recognize that your people are the keys to your success. You continually look for ways to recognize and reward them, while training and developing them to perform at higher levels.

| Grade: | 1 | 2 | 3 | 4 | 5 | 6 | 7 | 8 | 9 | 10 |

What are three things you could do on a regular basis to make your company a great place to work?

6. **Organizational Development:** You continually seek ways to organize and reorganize your business to use your people and resources at their highest and best levels.

| Grade: | 1 | 2 | 3 | 4 | 5 | 6 | 7 | 8 | 9 | 10 |

What three steps could you take immediately to ensure that your business operates more efficiently and effectively?

1. _____
2. _____
3. _____

Way to Wealth Workbook: Blueprints for Business Success

7. **Innovation:** You continually seek better, faster, cheaper, easier ways to serve your customers, continually improving your products and services.

Grade:	1	2	3	4	5	6	7	8	9	10

What three actions could you take immediately to develop and introduce new products and services that would keep your business on the cutting edge?

1. _____

2. _____

3. _____

Notes

Chapter 1. Business Blueprints

5. Seven Responsibilities of Leadership

There are seven things you do that determine your success or failure as a business owner and executive. Improvements in any one of these areas can lead to greater productivity, performance, and profitability.

1. **Set and achieve goals**. What are the three most important business goals for which you are responsible?

    1. _____
    2. _____
    3. _____

2. **Innovate and market**. What are three things you could do immediately to market your products and services more effectively?

    1. _____
    2. _____
    3. _____

3. **Solve problems and make decisions**. What are the three biggest problems you are facing in your business today and what actions can you take to solve them?

    1. _____
    2. _____
    3. _____

4. **Set priorities** for deploying people and resources. What are your top priorities in your business?

    1. _____
    2. _____
    3. _____

Way to Wealth Workbook: Blueprints for Business Success

5. **Focus and concentrate.** What are the three most important areas of your business where single-minded concentration could provide the highest payoff in results and profitability?

   1. _____

   2. _____

   3. _____

6. **Perform and get results.** What are the three most important results that are expected of you?

   1. _____

   2. _____

   3. _____

7. **Lead by example; set the standard.** What qualities or behaviors could you pursue or practice each day that would build commitment and morale in your company?

   1. _____

   2. _____

   3. _____

Notes

_____
_____
_____
_____
_____
_____
_____

6. How to Hire—Guidelines

Your business can grow and prosper only to the degree that you can find and hire the best people. Hiring is a special skill that you can master with practice. Here are some key points to keep in mind in any hiring situation.

1. **Selection is 95% of success**. The best companies have the best people. If you hire the wrong people, it is almost impossible to build a great company.
2. **Never hire as a solution to a problem**. Take your time and hire someone only when you are convinced that he or she is a good choice.
3. **Poor hiring is expensive**. It costs three to six times a person's annual salary to hire and then lose him or her.
4. **Think through the job**. The greater clarity you have before you begin the hiring process, the better decision you will make.

    a) **Results expected**: Exactly what do you want the person to accomplish?

    1. _____
    2. _____
    3. _____

    b) **Skills required**: What demonstrable skills will he or she need to get those results?

    1. _____
    2. _____
    3. _____

    c) **Personality attributes necessary**: What kind of personality will be ideal for this job and for your company?

    1. _____
    2. _____
    3. _____

Way to Wealth Workbook: Blueprints for Business Success

5. **Write out the job description.** List all the skills, qualities, and personality attributes of the perfect candidate for the job, in as much detail as possible.

   1. _____
   2. _____
   3. _____

6. **Cast a wide net.** Contact as many sources of job candidates as possible. Tell people inside and outside your company that you are looking for a particular type of person for this job.

   1. _____
   2. _____
   3. _____

7. **Use key factors.** There are certain factors that are key to improving the interviewing process:

   a) **Achievement history**: What has the candidate done? The only real predictor of future performance is past performance in a similar job.
   b) **Sense of urgency**: Find someone who is eager to start the job as soon as possible.
   c) **Intelligent questions**: The more questions a candidate asks about the job, the better a choice he or she is likely to be.
   d) **Rule of three**:
      Interview at least three candidates.
      Interview the person you like at least three times.
      Have at least three people interview the candidate.
      Check at least three résumés.

8. **Check résumés and references personally.** Phone and ask, "Would you hire this person again?" The answer will tell you a lot.

9. **Hire slow, fire fast.** If you realize that you have made a hiring mistake, admit it and get rid of the person quickly.

10. **Start new hires off right—keep them busy.** Give each new employee lots of work from the first day. This early experience sets the tone for the rest of the person's employment.

Chapter 1. Business Blueprints

7. Hiring the Best People

Identify the tasks that only you can do. Hire people to do everything else.

1. What are the three **most important** things you do in your work?

    1. _____
    2. _____
    3. _____

2. What are the three tasks that you **enjoy** the most?

    1. _____
    2. _____
    3. _____

3. What three things do you do that **contribute** the most to your results?

    1. _____
    2. _____
    3. _____

4. What three tasks would you **delegate** to others if you could?

    1. _____
    2. _____
    3. _____

5. Of all the **low-value** tasks that you do, which ones, if done by others, would free up the most time for you?

    1. _____
    2. _____
    3. _____

Way to Wealth Workbook: Blueprints for Business Success

6. If you had **no limits**, what jobs would you delegate to someone else?

    1. _____

    2. _____

    3. _____

7. What jobs are you going to **hire and fill** in the next 30–90 days?

    1. _____

    2. _____

    3. _____

What one person are you going to hire immediately as a result of this exercise?

_____

Notes

Chapter 1. Business Blueprints

8. How to Build a Top Team

There are certain qualities and characteristics of top-performing work teams that have been identified in worldwide research. The more of these principles you include in your business, the more productive and profitable you will be.

1. **Shared goals and objectives**: In a smoothly functioning team, everyone is clear about what the team is expected to accomplish. The goals of the team are shared and discussed by everyone. Each team member gives his or her input into how the goals and objectives can best be achieved. Each person feels like a part of the larger organization.

   Socrates said, "We only learn something by dialoging about it." There is a direct relationship between the amount of discussion a person engages in about the team's goals and the amount of commitment he or she has to achieving those goals.

   If you tell people what the goals of the team are and send them back to work, they will have a low level of commitment. When they experience problems or setbacks, they will give up easily or wait for you to come around and tell them what to do.

   But when you propose goals and objectives for the team and invite input and feedback from the members, when they go back to work, they will take "ownership" of those goals or objectives. They will feel a deeper level of commitment to achieving the goals and objectives than if they were not consulted at all.

   What are the three most important shared or common goals of your team?

   1. _____
   2. _____
   3. _____

2. **Shared values and principles**: With excellent teams, there is regular discussion about the values, principles, and behaviors that guide the decisions of the team. The leader encourages values such as honesty, openness, punctuality, responsibility for completing assignments, and quality work. Every member discusses and agrees on what they are.

Way to Wealth Workbook: Blueprints for Business Success

What are the most important values or principles that govern how you and your team work together?

1. _____

2. _____

3. _____

3. **Shared plans of action:** In this phase of team building, you go around the table and have each person explain exactly what part of the work he or she is going to accept responsibility for completing. At the end of this discussion, everyone knows what everyone else is going to be doing. Everyone knows how his or her work fits in with the work of the team.

   During this discussion about individual responsibilities, each person has a chance to ask each of the others about his or her assignment, how it will be measured, what results are expected from it, and when completion is due. The conversation is open, honest, and free-flowing. At the end, every team member knows his or her place on the team. Every team member knows how he or she fits into the big picture. Everyone feels like a valuable part of the organization.

   Make a list of all the people who work with you and then describe the most important things they do to contribute to the success of the company.

   Name   **Most Important Responsibilities**

   1. _____   _____

   2. _____   _____

   3. _____   _____

   4. _____   _____

   5. _____   _____

4. **Leadership**: There must always be a clear boss or leader in any organization. Democracy is a fine concept, but it goes only so far in business. Someone must be in command and take charge. And that someone is probably you.

   On a good team, every member knows who is in charge. The leader then sets an example for the others. The leader becomes the role model. If he or she expects people to do their assignments well and complete them on time, the leader leads by example and does his or her assignments well and on time, if not in advance.

Chapter 1. Business Blueprints

In addition, the leader of a business team has a special function. He or she is to act as a "blocker" and remove the obstacles that may hinder team members from doing their jobs. The job of the leader is to make sure each team member has the time, resources, equipment, and support necessary to do his or her job in an excellent fashion. The leader not only "leads the charge," but also makes sure that all the others are free to concentrate on doing the best job they possibly can.

What are your three most important leadership responsibilities?

1. _____

2. _____

3. _____

5. **Continuous review and evaluation:** In this final phase, the team regularly evaluates its progress from two perspectives.

   First, is the team getting the results that are expected by its customers or other parts of the company? In dealing with customers, the team sets up mechanisms to continually ask customers, "How are we doing?"

   The best businesses have a finger on the pulse of the customer at all times. They are continually asking their customers, in every way possible, directly and indirectly, for feedback. They are not afraid of criticism or negative responses. Top teams know that they can grow only if their customers are telling them honestly what they are doing or failing to do.

   What three ways do you measure customer satisfaction on an ongoing basis?

   1. _____

   2. _____

   3. _____

   The second area for evaluating progress has to do with the functioning of the team. Are all the members happy with the way they are working together? Are some members overloaded with work and others not busy enough? Are the values that the team has agreed on working? Is everyone satisfied?

   In the best businesses, disagreements are handled openly and honestly. If someone has a problem, he or she feels free to bring it up. The leader and the team accept responsibility for addressing the concerns of each team member. Everyone feels that all of them are in the same boat together.

Way to Wealth Workbook: Blueprints for Business Success

What are three ways you can ensure that all team members are happy with the way they are working together?

1. _____

2. _____

3. _____

Notes
_____
_____
_____
_____
_____
_____
_____
_____
_____
_____
_____
_____
_____
_____
_____
_____
_____

Chapter 1. Business Blueprints

9. How to Fire

The flipside of hiring is firing. More than two thirds of employees do not work out over time. When it is clear that the employee cannot or will not do the job, your responsibility is to let him or her go as soon as possible.

Firing is never easy, but it is necessary in building a business and in owning or managing a business. Your ability to fire people when it is clear they cannot or will not do the job you need done is a key business skill. Here are some guidelines:

1. The person who hires must also fire; this responsibility cannot be delegated.
2. Resolve to do what must be done; make a firm decision from which there is no turning back.
3. Prepare thoroughly. Ideally you should have given the employee at least two warnings that his or her performance must improve.
4. Always have a witness present. If you are firing a woman, always have a female employee as a witness. For a man, have a male employee as a witness.
5. Firing is best done early in the week, so the person can immediately start looking for another job, unless it is the end of the month.
6. Prepare the severance package in advance; know exactly what you are going to give the former employee.
7. Protect his or her self-esteem; do not rehash mistakes or failures. Refuse to discuss the past; it can only open you to argument and even a lawsuit. Keep your mouth shut and focus on letting the person go.
8. Be firm, but fair and unemotional. Do not become angry or accusatory.
9. Use the "broken record" method of firing, by repeating the words:

    "I have given this a lot of thought and I have decided that this is not the right job for you."

    "… and you are not the right person for this job."

    "… and I think you would be happier doing something else."

    Repeat these words until the employee accepts that your decision is final; then give him or her the severance package.
10. If the firing situation is negative or hostile, have someone accompany the former employee to his or her office to gather any personal belongings and leave the premises. Do not allow the former employee to access the computer.
11. Immediately change the locks on your doors, cancel all credit cards, and take whatever other protective measures that make sense.
12. Refuse to discuss the firing with other staff. Put it behind you and get on with the business.

41

10. Making the Firing Decision

Your ability to fire people when it is clear that they cannot or will not do the job you need done is a key business skill.

Here are some questions to answer when deciding on firing.

1. Is there anyone working for you, directly or indirectly, whom you would not hire or deal with again today, knowing what you know now?

    1. _____
    2. _____
    3. _____

2. What did you hire this person to do? What results did you expect from this person?

    1. _____
    2. _____
    3. _____

3. What mistakes has this person made? How has he or she failed to perform?

    1. _____
    2. _____
    3. _____

4. What does it cost you and others—both financially and emotionally—to have this person in this position?

    1. _____
    2. _____
    3. _____

Chapter 1. Business Blueprints

5. If you had the perfect person in this position, what results would you be getting?

    1. _____

    2. _____

    3. _____

6. What are the negative side effects of having an incompetent or unpleasant person in a key job?

    1. _____

    2. _____

    3. _____

7. How would it improve your life and your work if you got rid of this person and got the right person?

    1. _____

    2. _____

    3. _____

What one action are you going to take immediately as the result of your answers to the above questions?

_____

_____

_____

Notes

_____

_____

_____

_____

_____

11. Seven Qualities of Leadership

1. **Vision:** Leaders have a clear vision of the future of the business and they share it with everyone who works with the company. What is your vision for the future of your company? What would it look like if your company were great?

    1. _____

    2. _____

    3. _____

2. **Courage:** Leaders have the courage to take calculated risks with no guarantees of success, especially to fulfill the vision. In which areas do you need to take risks to make your vision a reality?

    1. _____

    2. _____

    3. _____

3. **Responsibility:** Leaders accept 100% responsibility for everything that happens and refuse to criticize, blame, or make excuses. What are your three most important responsibilities in your company?

    1. _____

    2. _____

    3. _____

4. **Integrity:** Leaders are completely honest with themselves and others. They get people to trust them by being trustworthy. Which are the three most important areas in your business that depend on your honesty and integrity to function well?

    1. _____

    2. _____

    3. _____

Chapter 1. Business Blueprints

5. **Commitment:** Leaders are totally committed to the success of the business. To which areas of your business are you most committed and to what outcomes?

   1. _____

   2. _____

   3. _____

6. **Concentration:** Leaders have developed the ability, through constant practice, to concentrate in those areas where the most important results are possible. In which three areas can single-minded concentration on your part bring about exceptional results?

   1. _____

   2. _____

   3. _____

7. **Excellence:** Leaders are committed to excellent work and excellent products and services. In which three areas is excellent performance the most important for the success of your business?

   1. _____

   2. _____

   3. _____

Notes

_____

_____

_____

_____

_____

_____

12. Seven Keys to Project Management

Business is made up of a series of projects. A project can be defined as a multi-task job. This is a series of tasks, each of which has to be completed in order to complete the project. Your ability to manage projects largely determines your level of success in business and in life in general.

Fortunately, there are several proven steps you can follow to increase the quality and quantity of your performance and output.

1. Start by clearly defining the **ideally completed project**. What are you trying to accomplish and what will the finished job look like?

    a) **Qualitatively**—the look, appearance, and quality of the project
    b) **Quantitatively**—the measurable results desired

2. Set the absolute **final date** for completion.

3. List every separate **task and function** within the project.

4. Organize the tasks in **order of importance**.

5. Organize the tasks in order of **time lines**.

    a) **Sequential**—tasks that must be done before other tasks are done or started
    b) **Parallel**—tasks that can be done or started at the same time

6. Determine the **limiting steps** or constraints that determine the speed of completion. What are the potential bottlenecks?

7. Assign **specific responsibility** for each task, complete with schedules, deadlines, and standards of performance.

Notes
_____
_____
_____
_____
_____

Chapter 1. Business Blueprints

13. Seven Questions for Any Investment

Business requires the continual investment of money. Your ability to think through and make intelligent decisions regarding investments of any kind can determine your success or failure. Here are the essential steps:

1. What exactly is the investment? How much is it and what is the money to be used for? Think on paper.
2. How much do you get back? What is the expected rate of return, the percentage? How sure is this return?
3. How is the return or profit to be generated? What are the exact steps to be followed to generate the projected amounts?
4. What is the worst possible outcome? What can possibly go wrong?
5. What alternative uses of the money exist? Are there better investments with higher or more certain returns?
6. How will this investment be measured and monitored? What accounting systems will be set up to track inputs and outcomes?
7. How comfortable do you feel about this investment? Do you have a high level of confidence in the people involved and in the logic of the investment? Trust your intuition.

Notes

CHAPTER TWO

Strategic Blueprints

Your most valuable asset is your ability to think. When you force yourself to ask and answer the key questions about yourself and your business, you make better decisions and get better results.

In this section, you will learn how to ask and answer the most important questions that determine business success. You can return to these questions over and over in the course of your business career, and you will often get different answers.

In this chapter:

1. Strategic Planning Questions	50
2. Business Planning Process	52
3. Ten Keys to Business Success	58
4. Seven Ways to Build an Entrepreneurial Business Faster	61
5. Your Core Business	63
6. The Driving Force in Strategy	65
7. Opportunity Analysis	67
8. Seven Steps to Business Profitability	69
9. Choosing the Right Location	71
10. Money and Financial Goals	79
11. Seven Steps to Problem Solving	80
12. Twelve Critical Orientations for Business and Personal Success	82
13. Time Allocation Exercise	85

WAY TO WEALTH WORKBOOK: BLUEPRINTS FOR BUSINESS SUCCESS

1. Strategic Planning Questions

When a company hires an expensive management consultant, these are the first questions he asks. Most people in positions of responsibility, including the owners, are unclear about the answers. As a result, they make poor decisions that can lead to lower profits, or even the failure of the business.

1. **What business are you in?** What business are you really in? Define your business in terms of what it *does* for your customers rather than what it *is* (your products or services).

   _____

   _____

2. **Who is your customer?** Who is your ideal customer? Who is your perfect customer? If you were to run an ad in the paper for perfect customers, how would you describe them?

   _____

   _____

3. **Why do your customers buy your products or services?** What value do they seek? What benefits do they desire? What change or improvement in their lives do they seek? What is the exact reason that would cause customers to buy from you immediately, rather than to delay the decision?

   _____

   _____

4. **What is your competitive advantage?** Your competitive advantage consists of one or more benefits that you offer your customers that no other competitor can offer. This is often called your "area of excellence" or "area of uniqueness."

   _____

   _____

5. **Who are your competitors?** Who does your ideal customer buy from them rather than from you? What advantages or benefits does your customer perceive that he or she receives in buying from your competitors that he or she does not feel that you provide?

   _____

   _____

Chapter 2. Strategic Blueprints

6. **What are the constraints that hold you back?** If your goal is to double your sales and profits over the next two or three years, what is holding you back from achieving that goal? Why aren't your sales twice as high *already*?

   _____

   _____

7. **What are the 20% of activities that you can engage in that could account for 80% of your results?** Who are the 20% of your customers who account for 80% of your business? What are the 20% of your products or services that account for 80% of your sales? What are the 20% of your products, services, and customers that account for 80% of your profits?

   1. 20% of activities? _____

   2. 20% of customers? _____

   3. 20% of products/services? _____

   4. 80% of your profits? _____

What actions are you going to take immediately as the result of your answers to the above questions?

   1. _____

   2. _____

   3. _____

Notes

_____

_____

_____

_____

_____

_____

_____

2. Business Planning Process

The most important step you can take at the beginning of a business venture and every year thereafter is to create a complete business plan. The exercise of asking and answering every question helps you to develop greater clarity about the business and what you need to do to ensure success.

The primary reason for business failure is the lack of a business plan. It is the first document asked for by venture capitalists. The development of the plan is a key measure of the competence of the business owner and the creation of the plan dramatically increases the ability of the owner to succeed.

The Business Plan

Section 1.0 Concept

In a few words, explain the reason for the business and both how and why you will generate profits from producing and selling the products and services you project. Explain why customers will buy from your company rather than from their current suppliers. What is different or special about your business idea?

_____

_____

_____

Section 2.0 Objectives

Explain your goals for sales, profitability, and return on investment, along with time lines and schedules for achieving these goals.

_____

_____

_____

Section 3.0 Market Analysis

Explain the market and how you intend to enter this market and earn a profit against entrenched competitors.

3.1. General description of the entire marketplace, for the product or service, including the total size of the market today:

_____

_____

Chapter 2. Strategic Blueprints

3.2. Precise description of market segment(s) or customer groups to be pursued:

3.3. Description of intermediate influences on buyers, such as dealers, distributors, sales representatives, associates, etc.:

3.4. Competitive conditions, present and anticipated—who else is selling to the customers you want?

3.5. Pricing conditions, present and anticipated—how much can you charge based on current offerings?

3.6. Governmental influences, present and anticipated—what sort of regulations and government departments and regulations will you have to deal with?

3.7. History of similar products, services, or businesses—who else is in this market and how well are they doing?

3.8. Breakeven point estimates—how many units and/or how much of the product or service must you sell each month to cover costs?

Section 4.0 Production

4.1. Equipment requirements—what will be required?

4.2. Facility requirements—what offices, warehouses, or manufacturing facilities will you need?

4.3. Raw materials, labor, and supplies—what are your requirements and what are your sources?

4.4. Quality control, packaging, transportation—what are they and how will they be arranged?

4.5. Program for initial time period—what steps will you have to take and in what order?

4.6. Schedule—who is to do what and by when?

4.7. Budget—series of financial projections showing how much money will be needed and when a return on that investment is to be expected:

4.8. Results expected—sales revenues and profitability estimates:

Chapter 2. Strategic Blueprints

4.9. Contingency plans—what will you do if you have unexpected delays in starting up and achieving profitability?

Section 5.0 Marketing

5.1. Method(s) of selling and advertising to be employed:

5.2. Product or service features and benefits to be emphasized—what makes your product or service superior to anything else on the market?

5.3. Program for initial time period—schedules to achieve sales targets:

5.4. Schedule—who is to do what and by when, who is responsible for performing specific functions and achieving specific goals?

5.5. Budget—for advertising, marketing, and sales:

5.6. Results expected—projections of sales and revenues:

5.7. Contingency plans—what will you do if you fail to meet your targets?

Section 6.0 Organization and People

6.1. Structure—who is accountable to whom and for what?

6.2. Staffing program for initial time period:

6.3. Schedule:

6.4. Budget:

6.5. Results expected—job descriptions and results expected from each person:

6.6. Contingency plans:

Section 7.0 Funds Flow and Financial Projections

7.1. Complete statement of expected sales and expenses for the next sales period:

7.2. Pro forma profit and loss statements—how much will you make or lose?

Chapter 2. Strategic Blueprints

7.3. Pro forma balance sheets—your cumulative profits or losses over the first one or two years:

_____

_____

7.4. Program for monitoring and controlling funds with people and systems included in the organization planning—how will you account for and report sources and uses of funds?

_____

_____

Section 8.0 Ownership

8.1. Summary of funding requirements—how much will you require?

_____

_____

8.2. Form of business—partnership, corporation, etc.:

_____

_____

8.3. Program for raising equity and/or debt money required, if any:

_____

_____

8.4. Projected returns to investors:

_____

_____

Summary

Every number, projection, and assumption in your business plan must be checked, double-checked, and verified. You must be prepared to explain and defend every statement and estimate with solid information based on market research and proof. Always begin by assuming that your numbers are incorrect, overly optimistic, or based on false information. Make every effort to disprove this negative assessment.

WAY TO WEALTH WORKBOOK: BLUEPRINTS FOR BUSINESS SUCCESS

3. Ten Keys to Business Success

There are ten keys to business success that you must incorporate into everything you do from the day you open your doors. The more accurately you can turn these keys, the greater is your likelihood of success. Lack of clarity or confusion in any one of these areas can be very costly.

1. **Key Purpose:** What is the purpose of a business? Many people think that the purpose of a business is to earn a profit, but they are wrong. The true purpose of a business is to *create and keep customers.* Profits are the result of creating and keeping a sufficient number of customers cost-effectively. What is your plan to create and keep customers?

   _____

   _____

2. **Key Measure:** The key measure of business success is *customer satisfaction.* Your ability to satisfy your customers to such a degree that they buy from you rather than from someone else, that they buy again, and that they bring their friends is the key determinant of growth and profitability. What are the most important areas of customer satisfaction in your business?

   1. _____
   2. _____
   3. _____

3. **Key Requirement:** The key requirement for wealth building and business success is for you to *add value* in some way. All wealth comes from adding value. All business growth and profitability come from adding value. Every day, you must be looking for ways to add more value to the customer experience. In what ways does your product, service, or business add value by improving the life or work of your customers?

   1. _____
   2. _____
   3. _____

Chapter 2. Strategic Blueprints

4. **Key Focus:** The most important person in the business is the *customer*. You must focus on the customer at all times. Customers are fickle, disloyal, changeable, impatient, and demanding—just like you. Nonetheless, the customer must be the central focus of everything you do in business. Who is your most important customer type and what must you do to please customers of this type?

    Customer type(s)? _____

    Keys to pleasing this type of customer?

    1. _____

    2. _____

    3. _____

5. **Key Word:** In life, work, and business, you will always be rewarded in direct proportion to the value of your *contribution* to others, as they see it. The focus on outward contribution, to your company, your customers, and your community, is the central requirement for you to become an ever more valuable person in every area. What are the most important contributions that you make to your business?

    1. _____

    2. _____

    3. _____

6. **Key Question:** The most important question you ask, to solve any problem, overcome any obstacle, or achieve any business goal is *"How?"* What are your three biggest problems or worries in your business today and actions could you take immediately to solve them?

Problem	**Solution**
1. _____	1. _____
2. _____	2. _____
3. _____	3. _____

Way to Wealth Workbook: Blueprints for Business Success

7. **Key Strategy:** In a world of rapid change and continuing, aggressive competition, you must practice *continuous improvement* in every area of your business and personal life. In what ways could you offer your products and services in a better, faster, cheaper, easier-to-use manner?

    1. _____

    2. _____

    3. _____

8. **Key Activity:** The heartbeat of your business is sales. Dun & Bradstreet analyzed thousands of companies that had gone broke over the years and concluded that the #1 reason for business failure was "low sales." When they researched further, they found that the #1 reason for business success was "high sales." And all else was commentary. What steps could you take immediately to increase your sales?

    1. _____

    2. _____

    3. _____

9. **Key Number:** The most important number in business is *cash flow*. Cash flow is to the business as blood and oxygen are to the brain. You can have every activity working efficiently in your business, but if your cash flow is cut off for any reason, the business can die, sometimes overnight. What could you do immediately to increase your cash flow?

    1. _____

    2. _____

    3. _____

10. **Key Goal:** Every business must have a *growth plan*. Growth must be the goal of all of your business activities. You should have a goal to grow 10%, 20%, or even 30% each year. Some companies grow 50% and 100% per year, and not by accident. What are three things that you could do to grow your business faster?

    1. _____

    2. _____

    3. _____

Chapter 2. Strategic Blueprints

4. Seven Ways to Build an Entrepreneurial Business Faster

You must be continually seeking better, cheaper, faster ways to build your business. Here are the seven best ways:

1. Acquire more customers at **lower costs**. What could you do to attract more customers at a lower cost?

    1. _____
    2. _____
    3. _____

2. Stimulate more **frequent purchases** and resales by expanding your variety of offerings. What could you offer your customers to cause them to buy from you more often?

    1. _____
    2. _____
    3. _____

3. Achieve larger sales per customer via **up-selling and cross-selling**. How could you up-sell and cross-sell more effectively?

    1. _____
    2. _____
    3. _____

4. Deliver your product or service at **lower cost** through greater efficiency. How could you increase the efficiency of your business operations?

    1. _____
    2. _____
    3. _____

Way to Wealth Workbook: Blueprints for Business Success

5. Get **more and better referrals** to new customers, lowering your cost of advertising and sales. How could you solicit or stimulate more referrals from your customers?

    1. _____

    2. _____

    3. _____

6. Build **better customer relationships** and create more loyal, appreciative customers. What could you do to raise levels of customer satisfaction?

    1. _____

    2. _____

    3. _____

7. Increase the **speed of the sales process** by using better, faster, more efficient sales skills and methods. How could you increase your ability to sell in your business?

    1. _____

    2. _____

    3. _____

Notes

_____
_____
_____
_____
_____
_____

Chapter 2. Strategic Blueprints

5. Your Core Business

Your core business is the main source of your sales and profits. **Focus and concentration** on the core are the keys to sales, success, and profitability.

1. What is your **core business**? What is it that you do or provide that customers appreciate and pay for the most?

    1. _____
    2. _____
    3. _____

2. What are your **most popular** products and services, the easiest to sell?

    1. _____
    2. _____
    3. _____

3. What are your **key skills and competencies**, personally and as a business, that enable you to sell to and service your core business?

    1. _____
    2. _____
    3. _____

4. What are your **"areas of superiority,"** compared with your competitors, in your core business?

    1. _____
    2. _____
    3. _____

5. Who are your **core customers** for your core business? Who are the 20% who buy 80% of what you sell?

    1. _____
    2. _____
    3. _____

Way to Wealth Workbook: Blueprints for Business Success

6. What are the **greatest opportunities** for you to expand your core business?

    1. _____

    2. _____

    3. _____

7. Who are your core **people** in your business today?

    1. _____

    2. _____

    3. _____

8. What could you do to get **more and better sales** and financial results from developing your core business even more?

    1. _____

    2. _____

    3. _____

What one action are you going to take immediately to exploit your core products, services, strengths, customers, and markets?

_____

_____

Notes

_____

_____

_____

_____

_____

_____

Chapter 2. Strategic Blueprints

6. The Driving Force in Strategy

Your **driving force** determines the central focus and area of concentration of your business. You must select your driving force with care.

Each company must be concerned about more than one of these areas, but it must be clear which driving force is dominant. A company can only have one central focus. What is yours?

1. **Market Needs:** The focus is on serving a particular market with whatever it needs. What are your main markets for what you sell?

    1. _____
    2. _____
    3. _____

2. **Product/Service:** The focus is on selling greater quantities of a specific product or service at higher prices. What are your specific products or services?

    1. _____
    2. _____
    3. _____

3. **Method of Sale/Distribution:** The focus is on selling more products or services via a specific channel. How do you get your products or services to your customers?

    1. _____
    2. _____
    3. _____

4. **Return/Profit:** The focus is on achieving a specific level of profit from sales, irrespective of product or service sold. What are your profit goals for your business—gross, net, and margin?

    1. _____
    2. _____
    3. _____

5. **Growth/Market Share:** The focus is on achieving a specific rate of growth or share of market. What are your goals to grow your business in the years ahead?

   1. _____

   2. _____

   3. _____

6. **Technology:** Marketing strategy is determined by technological capabilities and strengths. What are the key technologies that determine your business activities?

   1. _____

   2. _____

   3. _____

7. **Manufacturing:** Strategy is determined by manufacturing capability and facilities. How do you produce the products or services you sell?

   1. _____

   2. _____

   3. _____

Which one of the driving forces above is most important to you and your business operations? Your correct choice of your driving force determines the entire direction of your business.

_____

_____

Notes

Chapter 2. Strategic Blueprints

7. Opportunity Analysis

Throughout your business life, especially when you are financially successful, you will be presented with opportunities to **invest** your time and money in additional money-making opportunities.

By the law of probability, **90% or more** of these opportunities will be not worth pursuing. They will only be opportunities for you to lose money.

When you are presented with an "opportunity," your first task is to remain completely **unemotional** and detached, exactly as if you are acting as a consultant or advisor to someone else. Your job is to ask the right questions and analyze the opportunity carefully before you make a commitment.

Remember: the only thing easy about money is **losing** it. Here are seven steps to ensure that you don't lose money.

1. Determine the **nature of the opportunity**. What exactly is the business proposition in terms of the amount required, your personal involvement, and the expected return on investment?

2. Determine the **probability of success**. What is the percentage of probability that it will be successful?

3. Determine the **investment required**. Exactly how much will you have to put in, now and in the future?

4. Determine the **time required**. How much of your time will be needed and how long will it take until you get the profit projected?

Way to Wealth Workbook: Blueprints for Business Success

5. Determine the **people and resources required**. How many hours of your time and that of others will be necessary and how much will this cost?

   _____

   _____

6. Determine how **committed** you are. On a scale of 1–10, how excited are you about this opportunity and how much do you believe in it?

   _____

   _____

7. Determine the **other options available**. What are all the other ways and places in which you could invest the same amount of time and money?

   _____

   _____

You should proceed on a business opportunity only if you are confident about all the projections and you are satisfied with your answers to the above question.

Notes

_____

_____

_____

_____

_____

_____

_____

_____

_____

_____

Chapter 2. Strategic Blueprints

8. Seven Steps to Business Profitability

There are seven steps to business **profitability**: an improvement in any one of these numbers can improve your profitability immediately.

1. The number of **prospects** you attract with your marketing activities. How could you attract more and better prospects?

    1. _____
    2. _____
    3. _____

2. The number of prospects you **convert** to customers. How could you improve your conversion rates?

    1. _____
    2. _____
    3. _____

3. The number of **individual sales** you make. How could you improve your sales ability?

    1. _____
    2. _____
    3. _____

4. The **average size** of each sale. How could you get your customers to buy more each time?

    1. _____
    2. _____
    3. _____

5. The **average cost** per sale. How could you reduce your costs?

    1. _____
    2. _____
    3. _____

Way to Wealth Workbook: Blueprints for Business Success

6. The **profit margin** or percentage you earn on each sale. How could you increase your profit per sale?

   1. _____

   2. _____

   3. _____

7. How often you **resell** each customer. How could you get your customers to buy from you more often?

   1. _____

   2. _____

   3. _____

Any improvement in any one of these numbers will increase your profits. Improvements in several numbers at the same time can increase your profits substantially.

Notes

Chapter 2. Strategic Blueprints

9. Choosing the Right Location

One of the most important parts of the marketing mix, the critical determinant of business success or failure, is your place of business. You must take the time to decide upon the very best place of business for your particular enterprise, your geographical location, where you interact with your customers and make sales. What is your current place of business?

_____
_____

The **"place"** refers to that point where your customers come face to face or voice to voice with your product or service and makes the decision to purchase it. Your choice of a place or location of business can make or break you. You must select it with care. In what other ways do you communicate with your customers and make sales?

1. _____
2. _____
3. _____

Make It Easy to Buy

Human beings are lazy by nature. They seek comfort, convenience, and ease of purchase. Customers want to satisfy their needs in the fastest and easiest way possible. They will pay more money, and pay it faster, for a product or service that is easy to acquire, easy to use, and easy to consume. You must satisfy this need for convenience above all other things. How can you make it more convenient for your customers to buy from you?

1. _____
2. _____
3. _____

Fish Where the Fish Are

There is a saying, "Fish where the fish are." This means that your choice of a location or way of providing your products and services to your business has to be **convenient and accessible** to the greatest number of potential customers. You must carefully consider this factor before you make your final choice of your place of business or your main distribution channel. Where is your largest concentration of potential customers?

1. _____

2. _____

3. _____

In retail business, in shopping areas, streets, or malls, the most important determinant of sales will be the number of people who walk past the front of your store. The next most important determinant will be how open and inviting your store appears. How attractive does it look to a passerby? *How much does it invite a passerby to enter and look around?*

_____

_____

Store layout and design, colors, lighting, openness, and space are critical factors in creating the kind of comfort level that people need to buy a product or service from you.

1. _____

2. _____

3. _____

The Correct Side of the Street

If you have a retail establishment that depends on people driving by your location, you must be careful about which side of the street you choose. When I began doing real estate development, I learned to my surprise that there is both a "drive-to-work" side and a "drive-home" side of every business street or main artery. How suitable is your current location?

_____

_____

People don't stop to shop on their way to work, only on their way home. Many beautifully designed and well-built strip shopping centers fail in the market because they are on the wrong side of the street. Many average-looking strip shopping centers are booming with business because they are on the "drive-home" side of the street. They are located in such a way that it makes it easy for

Chapter 2. Strategic Blueprints

the customer to buy. *How can you locate your business activities to make it easier for the customer to buy from you?*

Credibility Is Essential

J. Paul Getty wrote a book many years ago entitled How to Be Rich. At that time, he was one of the richest men in the world. In the book, he advised young entrepreneurs to get an office or other location on the most prestigious street in their city or town—and, if possible, in one of the most prestigious buildings on the best-known street, even if only the size of a broom closet.

The most important word in business is "credibility." By locating on a well-known street in a well-known building, you have instant credibility. As soon as people hear about your address, they immediately grade you higher and better as a business and as a businessperson than if you were located in a suburb or on a side street. Where could you locate your business so that your address would give you instant credibility?

Go with the Flow

There is a "small town" versus "large city" mentality in business. What this means is that, in the main, people do not go from large cities to make their purchases in small towns, unless there are very good reasons.

In the seminar, speaking, and training business, we have found that people will come from small towns to the big city to attend a training seminar, but very few people will go from the big city to a small town for the same reason.

Whenever we work with promoters and seminar organizers, we encourage them to establish their head office in the biggest city in the state or country. In every case, without fail, where one of our representatives has decided to locate in a small town, the business has eventually failed. The majority of customers, who live in the large cities, don't take a business or a supplier located in a small town seriously. It has insufficient credibility. How could you set up an address and telephone number in the heart of the biggest city in your market area, even if your actual location is in a smaller town?

Different Strokes for Different Folks

If you operate a fast-food outlet of any kind, you must be located on a high-traffic road or street. Fast food is an impulse buy. People stop to order fast food because they see the fast-food location at the same time as they feel the pangs of hunger. In many cases, drivers will turn into the first fast-food outlet they see when they decide they want to eat.

If you operate a sit-down restaurant, a drive-by location may be helpful if you are selling low-cost, convenience foods, such as T.G.I.Friday's or California Pizza Kitchen. These outlets are dependent on drive-by traffic and ease of access for their business. Is your product or service an impulse buy?

On the other hand, if you are a first-class restaurant offering high-quality, high-priced specialty foods, you can locate in an out-of-the-way place and be successful on the basis of customer satisfaction and word-of-mouth advertising. People will seek out an excellent restaurant, no matter where it is located. Do people patronize your business because of your high-quality products or services?

If you sell your products wholesale to retail outlets or other distributors, you should locate in a business, commercial, or industrial area with ample access and egress for both your suppliers and your customers. As a wholesale provider, you do not need special signage or drive-by visibility. Your customers are going to come to you as a result of the products you provide and your marketing efforts.

Questions You Must Ask

There are a series of questions you must ask and answer, over and over again, in determining where you are going to make your products and services available to the greatest number of customers. As markets and customers change their demands and preferences, you may have to revisit these questions on a regular basis.

Chapter 2. Strategic Blueprints

1. **Who is your customer?** The more accurately you describe your exact, ideal customer for exactly what you sell, the more easily you can determine where to locate your place of business.

    1. _____
    2. _____
    3. _____

2. **Where are your customers?** Are they in your neighborhood? Are they in your part of the city? Are they located everywhere in your city or urban area? Are they statewide, nationwide, or international?

    You can ask where your customers are located in terms of the type of businesses in which they work. Your customers could be people at certain positions at certain levels of a particular organization. Where are they?

    1. _____
    2. _____
    3. _____

Determine Your Sales Territory

Another answer to "Where is my customer?" can be the geographical area in which you sell. This is often defined as your "sales territory." This is the area for which you are responsible and from which you will get more than 90% of your customers. What is your territory? Are there different ways and places that you could offer your products for sale?

1. _____
2. _____
3. _____

1. **Where do your customers live?** Where do your customers work? You know that people prefer ease and convenience over almost anything else. They like to shop

nearby. Is there any way that you could move your business closer to your customers to make it easier for them to do business with you?

1. _____

2. _____

3. _____

2. **What similar products or services do your potential customers buy elsewhere?**
   Could you locate your place of business where customers for what you sell come and buy from someone else?

   1. _____

   2. _____

   3. _____

3. **What kind of strategic alliances or host-beneficiary relationships could you create with businesses that are not competing with you?**

   One of the best business strategies you can pursue is the formation of strategic alliances or host-beneficiary relationships.

   In a strategic alliance, you arrange with a noncompeting provider of products and services that is already selling to your ideal type of customers, so you can sell your products or services to their customers. At the same time, you encourage your customers to buy from them. This is a symbiotic relationship that benefits both parties, at no cost to either.

   In a host-beneficiary relationship, you offer something free or at a considerable discount to the customers of another company that sells a noncompeting product or service to the same kind of customers you wish to attract. In this way, it appears as though the host is giving a benefit to its customers by sending them to you for something that is free or deeply discounted. What could you offer free to the customers of a company who could be your customers as well?

   1. _____

   2. _____

   3. _____

Chapter 2. Strategic Blueprints

4. **Where do your customers shop?** Human beings are creatures of habit. They get into a rhythm of shopping in a particular way, at a particular place, and then they continue to shop that way for the indefinite future.

   1. _____
   2. _____
   3. _____

   By identifying exactly who your customers are and exactly what they want, you can then look around and find out where your ideal type of customer is currently shopping. This can lead you to either locating "where the fish are" or to advertising in that area to attract those specific shoppers to your place of business or to your products or services.

5. **What other stores or outlets could carry your products as well?** In other words, where else could you sell your products and services? Who else could sell your products and services for you? What other stores could carry your products or services along with what they are currently offering?

   1. _____
   2. _____
   3. _____

Be Visible to Your Customers

Something as simple as high-quality signage can have a major impact on your sales. It should be visible far enough away so that passing motorists can see it and then get to your place of business. When driving on the highway, you will often see signs that announce a restaurant or other business a few miles ahead. Sometimes the signs indicate how to get to the business. They make it easy to find the business and easy to get there.

Keep looking for ways to make it easier and more convenient to buy from you. Remember: customers are selfish, impatient, fickle, and disloyal. They will buy from whoever offers them the products and services they want, at prices they are willing to pay, the fastest and easiest way possible. What steps could you take immediately to improve your location relative to your customers?

1. _____

2. _____

3. _____

Your decisions about where you locate your business, and how you make it easier to buy from you, can have a major impact on how much you sell, and how profitable your business becomes.

Notes

Chapter 2. Strategic Blueprints

10. Money and Financial Goals

You can't hit a target you can't see. The greater clarity you develop regarding the money you want to make and keep in the course of your business life, the more likely it is that you will achieve these goals.

Take the time to think through your **financial goals**, for yourself and your business, your family, your future and your dreams.

- How much do you want to **earn** each year? _____
- How much do you want to **save or invest** each month (as an amount or percentage of income)? _____
- How much do you want to have each year as **after-tax income** when you retire? _____
- How much do you want to have saved and invested when you **retire**? _____
- How much do you need to **provide** for your children and for their education? _____
- How much **insurance** do you need to provide for those who depend on you? _____
- When and how do you intend to be **debt-free**? _____

Based on your answers to the above questions, write out five goals for yourself for the next three to five years, as if you had no limitations on the amounts you could earn and save:

Goals   **Amounts Required**

1. _____   _____

2. _____   _____

3. _____   _____

What one action are you going to take immediately to begin moving toward the accomplishments of your most important financial goals?

_____

_____

11. Seven Steps to Problem Solving

Your life and business will be a continuous series of problems and difficulties. They never end. They come steadily, like the waves of the ocean, one after the other.

Your ability to solve the problems you meet on a daily basis is the critical determinant of your ability to succeed in business or in life. The better you get at solving problems, the more powerful and effective you will feel.

When you develop the habit of approaching each problem with a systematic method, you become better and better at solving them. Here are the seven steps:

1. Approach the problem **confidently**. Assume there is a logical, positive solution.

2. Define the problem **clearly**—in writing.

3. Change your language; call it a "situation," a "challenge," or, even better, an "opportunity."

4. Ask, "What are all the possible **causes** of this situation?"

5. Ask, "What are all the possible solutions to this situation?"

6. Make a decision. **Any** solution is usually better than no solution.

Chapter 2. Strategic Blueprints

7. Assign specific **responsibility** to someone and set a deadline for action.

After you have met and mastered a problem of any kind, ask yourself, "What are the valuable lessons contained in this problem?"

When you review a problem and look for what you can learn from it, you become smarter and more capable of solving even greater problems in the future.

Notes

12. Twelve Critical Orientations for Business and Personal Success

The greatest discovery in human history, the basis of all religions, philosophy, and psychology, is that, *you become what you think about, most of the time.*

Successful business people think better than their competitors. Based on interviews with thousands of entrepreneurs, we find that they think differently in 12 areas:

1. **Future Orientation:** Top people think about the future most of the time. If your life and business were perfect five years from now, what would it look like?

    1. _____
    2. _____
    3. _____

2. **Goal Orientation:** Top people think about their goals most of the time. What goals, if you achieved them, would have the greatest positive impact on your life?

    1. _____
    2. _____
    3. _____

3. **Result Orientation:** Top people think about results most of the time. What results, if you achieved them, would help you the most?

    1. _____
    2. _____
    3. _____

4. **Solution Orientation:** Top people think about solutions most of the time. What are your three biggest problems or worries in life right now?

    1. _____
    2. _____
    3. _____

Chapter 2. Strategic Blueprints

What are the three most simple and direct solutions to these problems?

1. _____
2. _____
3. _____

5. **Excellence Orientation:** Top people think about quality and excellent performance most of the time. They are determined to be the best at what they do. What actions could you take to increase the quality of your products or services immediately?

   1. _____
   2. _____
   3. _____

6. **People Orientation:** Top people think about the quality of their personal and business relationships much of the time.

   Who are the three most important people in your business or financial life?

   1. _____
   2. _____
   3. _____

   Who are the three most important people in your personal life?

   1. _____
   2. _____
   3. _____

7. **Customer Orientation:** Top business people think about their customers, and how they can satisfy them better, most of the time. Who are your most important customers?

   1. _____
   2. _____
   3. _____

Way to Wealth Workbook: Blueprints for Business Success

8. **Sales Orientation:** Top business owners think about sales most of the time. What are your three most important ways to generate sales?

    1. _____

    2. _____

    3. _____

9. **Growth Orientation:** Top people are continually learning, growing, and improving personally and professionally. What are the three most common ways that you acquire new knowledge and skill?

    1. _____

    2. _____

    3. _____

10. **Health Orientation:** Top people take excellent care of their physical health. What are the three most important things you do to remain healthy?

    1. _____

    2. _____

    3. _____

11. **Profit Orientation:** Top businesspeople think about the profitability of every business activity. What are the three most profitable things you sell, deliver, or do?

    1. _____

    2. _____

    3. _____

12. **Action Orientation:** All successful people are intensely action oriented. What three actions should you take immediately as the result of your answers to the above questions?

    1. _____

    2. _____

    3. _____

13. Time Allocation Exercise

You cannot save time; you can only spend it differently. To manage your time and your life more effectively, you must be continually asking what you should be doing more, less, starting, or stopping.

Business and Career

1. What are you going to do **more**?

    1. _____

    2. _____

    3. _____

2. What are you going to do **less**?

    1. _____

    2. _____

    3. _____

3. What are you going to **start** doing?

    1. _____

    2. _____

    3. _____

4. What are you going to **stop** doing?

    1. _____

    2. _____

    3. _____

What single action are you going to take immediately?

_____

_____

Way to Wealth Workbook: Blueprints for Business Success

Family and Relationships

1. What are you going to do **more**?

    1. _____

    2. _____

    3. _____

2. What are you going to do **less**?

    1. _____

    2. _____

    3. _____

3. What are you going to **start** doing?

    1. _____

    2. _____

    3. _____

4. What are you going to **stop** doing?

    1. _____

    2. _____

    3. _____

What single action are you going to take immediately?
_____
_____

Money and Investments

1. What are you going to do **more**?

    1. _____

    2. _____

    3. _____

Chapter 2. Strategic Blueprints

2. What are you going to do **less**?

   1. _____

   2. _____

   3. _____

3. What are you going to **start** doing?

   1. _____

   2. _____

   3. _____

4. What are you going to **stop** doing?

   1. _____

   2. _____

   3. _____

What single action are you going to take immediately?

_____

_____

Health and Fitness

1. What are you going to do **more**?

   1. _____

   2. _____

   3. _____

2. What are you going to do **less**?

   1. _____

   2. _____

   3. _____

3. What are you going to **start** doing?

   1. _____

   2. _____

   3. _____

4. What are you going to **stop** doing?

   1. _____

   2. _____

   3. _____

What single action are you going to take immediately?
_____
_____

Notes

CHAPTER THREE

Marketing Blueprints

Marketing is the core skill of successful business. Your ability to attract interested prospects to consider your products or services is the key skill of entrepreneurship.

Marketing is different from selling. Marketing is the process of identifying who your ideal customer is, and what he or she will buy. You then design your products or services so that they are ideally suited to the current marketplace. This means that what you sell has a distinct and desirable competitive advantage that makes is superior in some way to anything else that is available.

The second part of marketing is to tell potential customers what you have, and how it can satisfy a need, solve a problem, or achieve a goal for the customer. This embraces public relations, advertising, and promotion of all kinds—aimed at attracting the attention of the customer.

Customers today are bombarded with 4,000 advertisements or commercial messages each day. Your job is to find a way to stand out from them and get the customer to pay attention to you. Everything you do in marketing must be aimed at this result.

As always, the better you think and plan, the better decisions you will make. One change in your marketing strategy can transform your business, boost your sales, and increase your profits.

Way to Wealth Workbook: Blueprints for Business Success

In this chapter:

1. Seven Keys to Marketing Success	91
2. Seven Questions for Market Planning	93
3. Four Principles of Marketing Strategy	95
4. Seven P's of the Marketing Mix	101
5. Finding a New Product or Service	104
6. How to Do Fast, Cheap Market Research	107
7. Nine Great Marketing Questions	109
8. Seven Reasons Why People Buy Things	112
9. Key Concerns in Making a Buying Decision	114
10. Becoming the Quality Choice	116
11. Buying Customers—Determining Your Costs of Acquisition	120
12. Lifetime Value of a Customer	121
13. How to Write Effective Advertising	122
14. 24 Ways to Sell Your Product or Service	125

Chapter 3. Marketing Blueprints

1. Seven Keys to Marketing Success

You must ask and answer these questions over and over throughout your business career. A single change in one of your answers can change your entire business. In addition, because of our fast-paced business climate, you must always be open to the possibility that what you are doing right now is completely wrong.

1. **Specialization:** You must specialize in a type of customer, a particular product or service, or a geographical area. What is your specialization?

    1. Type of customer? _____
    2. Product or service? _____
    3. Geographical area? _____

2. **Differentiation:** You must be superior to your competitors in some way. How are your products or services better than others'?

    1. _____
    2. _____
    3. _____

3. **Segmentation:** You must identify the very best customers for what you sell, the ones who most appreciate your areas of specialization and differentiation. Who are they? Describe them in detail.

    1. _____
    2. _____
    3. _____

4. **Concentration:** You must focus all your marketing, advertising, and sales efforts on your best potential customers. How can you do this?

    1. _____
    2. _____
    3. _____

5. **Positioning:** You must own certain words or ideas in your customers' minds. What words do you want people to use when they talk about you?

   1. _____

   2. _____

   3. _____

6. **Branding:** This is the value that customers associate with your products or services that make them more valuable than those of your competitors. What is your brand image in the mind of your market?

   1. _____

   2. _____

   3. _____

7. **Strategy and tactics:** These are the specific actions you are going to take to market in order to sell more of your products and services. What steps can you take immediately to be more successful in your market?

   1. _____

   2. _____

   3. _____

Notes

_____

_____

_____

_____

_____

_____

_____

Chapter 3. Marketing Blueprints

2. Seven Questions for Market Planning

Peter Drucker, the most important management thinker of his age, suggested that these seven questions were the most important for a business owner to ask and answer on a regular basis.

The questions are simple, but most business owners are not able to answer them accurately. In addition, these answers will change as your business grows and evolves. One wrong answer here can be very expensive.

1. **What business are you really in?**

    What business are you in today? _____

    What business will you be in if current trends continue? _____

    What business should you be in? _____

    What business could you be in? _____

    Describe your business in terms of what you do for customers. _____

2. **Who is your customer?** Whom do you have to satisfy? Describe him or her accurately:

    1. _____
    2. _____
    3. _____

3. **What does your customer consider value?** What specific benefits does your customer get from using your products or services?

    1. _____
    2. _____
    3. _____

4. **What do you do especially well?** What is your area of superiority? What is your competitive advantage?

    1. _____
    2. _____
    3. _____

WAY TO WEALTH WORKBOOK: BLUEPRINTS FOR BUSINESS SUCCESS

5. **What are your core competencies?** What should they be? What could they be? In what parts of your business are you talented and skilled?

   1. _____

   2. _____

   3. _____

6. What are or could be the **10–20% of your activities** that could account for 80–90% of your results?

   1. _____

   2. _____

   3. _____

7. What are the **critical constraints** on your ability to achieve your goals? What is holding you back from greater success?

   1. _____

   2. _____

   3. _____

What specific actions are suggested by the answers to the above questions?

   1. _____

   2. _____

   3. _____

Chapter 3. Marketing Blueprints

3. Four Principles of Marketing Strategy

The four principles of marketing strategy are the keys to business success or failure. Your ability to ask and answer these questions, and to make whatever changes the market demands, will largely determine your success or failure.

1. Specialization

You must decide in exactly what area of your product or service market you are going to specialize. You cannot be all things to all customers.

Too many businesses make the mistake of trying to offer too many products or services to too many types of customers at too many prices in too many ways. This is not the way to wealth.

You can specialize in three fundamental areas—product/service, customer/market, or geographical location. What are the ways that you can specialize, rather than generalize?

1. _____

2. _____

3. _____

You can specialize in a product/service area. This is what you do when you decide on a single or a limited number of particular products or services that you are going to provide to your market. You can specialize in hardware, hot dogs, or hard-to-find books. Both you and your customers must be clear about your area of product/service specialization. What products or service do you specialize in offering?

1. _____

2. _____

3. _____

You can specialize in serving a specific customer or market. All-State Legal Supply of New Jersey specializes in law firms, providing them with every product they need to operate efficiently. Wal-Mart specializes in serving customers

95

who live from paycheck to paycheck. McDonald's specializes on providing fast food for people who want to eat quickly and conveniently. What customers do you specialize in serving?

1. _____

2. _____

3. _____

You can specialize in a particular geographical area. This can be your neighborhood, your city, your state, the country, or the entire world. When you choose to specialize in a particular area, you are choosing not to offer your products or services outside that area.

This is often the case for franchise operations or for companies offering exclusive products and services in a particular market. In business, deciding what to do is equally as important as deciding what not to do. When you are clear about your area of specialization, it is much easier for you to make decisions about the right and wrong products and services to offer to your customers. In what geographical area do you specialize?

1. _____

2. _____

3. _____

2. Differentiation

This is perhaps the most important strategic marketing principle. All business success requires a differentiation of some kind. All business success requires that you be both different and better than your competitors in some clear, distinct way. What makes you different and better than your competition?

1. _____

2. _____

3. _____

Your area of differentiation is called your **"competitive advantage."** Your competitive advantage is what makes your product or service superior to those of your competitors. It is what makes what you offer better than what another company offers. Sometimes this is called your "area of excellence." You develop a

Chapter 3. Marketing Blueprints

competitive advantage by becoming absolutely excellent in some area that is so important to your potential customers that they will buy from you rather than from someone else. What are your areas of excellence in your business?

1. _____
2. _____
3. _____

Perhaps the most important part of competitive advantage is your **"unique selling proposition."** This is the one benefit you offer for dealing with you that no other competitor can offer. It is **unique**. No one else has it, in any way. It represents a value that customers are willing to pay for rather than do business with your competitors. What is your unique selling proposition?

1. _____
2. _____
3. _____

If you don't have a competitive advantage, you must develop one. In addition, you must look into the future and determine what competitive advantage you must offer in the months and years ahead to be seen as one of the best companies in your market.

Your goal is to offer products and services in such a way that you are seen to be in the top 10% of suppliers in your market. Your goal is to be "the best." The process of achieving competitive advantage requires a commitment to **"continuous and never-ending improvement."**

3. Segmentation

The third strategic marketing principle requires that you segment your market. You divide up your prospective customers into separate groups, based on the product or service area in which you specialize and the areas of superiority that you offer to prospective customers. What are your best market segments?

1. _____
2. _____
3. _____

97

In market segmentation, you clearly identify those customers who are **ideal for what you sell** and who most appreciate and are willing to pay for those aspects of your product or service that make your offerings superior to those of your competitors.

In market segmentation, you begin with a description of your ideal or perfect customer. If you could wave a magic wand and attract the perfect customers to you, what would they look like? How would you describe them?

Define Your Target Market

Who is your *ideal* customer? Age? Income? Education? Position or occupation? Industry? Geographical location? Type of family? Interests? Desires? Ambitions? Problems?

1. _____

2. _____

3. _____

Once you have identified your ideal customer, this becomes your *target market*. Describe your perfect customer: _____

_____

You then ask questions such as these:

- Where is my perfect customer? _____

- When does he or she buy? _____

- How does he or she buy? _____

- What value does he or she seek in buying from me? _____

_____

- Of all the benefits my product or service offers, what is the one benefit that is most important to my ideal customer? _____

_____

Determine Your Competition

Who are your competitors? Why doesn't your ideal customer buy from you? Why does your ideal customer buy from your competitors? What value does your ideal customer see in buying from your competitors that he or she does not

Chapter 3. Marketing Blueprints

see in buying from you? What could you do to offset this perception? List your major and minor competitors for what you sell.

1. _____

2. _____

3. _____

Creating and keeping customers is difficult, complex, frustrating, and time-consuming. Customers are demanding, fickle, disloyal and unpredictable. They always want the very most for the very least and they want it immediately. They will abandon a supplier they've used for 20 years if they perceive something better or cheaper across the street.

The only hope you have in acquiring customers is to focus most of your time and attention on determining exactly who they are, where they are, and what you have to do to get them to buy from you rather than from someone else.

Segment Your Market

If you offer more than one product or service, you will have to divide your potential customers into separate market segments. You will then have to identify the characteristics and qualities of prospective customers in each of these segments in order to advertise and sell to them effectively.

Keep asking these questions:

- Who are my customers?
- Where are my customers?
- Why do they buy?
- When do they buy?
- How do they buy?
- How can I get them to buy from me rather than from someone else?
- What value do they have to perceive that they will get from me that they will not get from anyone else?

Failing to ask and answer these questions accurately can damage or even destroy your business.

Who is the perfect customer for what you sell?

1. _____

2. _____

3. _____

4. Concentration

Once you have applied the principles of specialization, differentiation, and segmentation to your products and services and to your customers and markets, you now have to concentrate your limited resources. You have to focus your time, energy, and money on those prospective customers that you have identified who are the most likely to buy from you the soonest.

In concentrating your resources, you identify the advertising media and promotional methods most likely to attract and influence the people who are most likely to buy from you immediately. How could you concentrate all your marketing, advertising, and sales resources on the best potential customers for what you sell?

1. _____
2. _____
3. _____

What changes are you going to make immediately in your marketing activities based on your answers to the above?

1. _____
2. _____
3. _____

Notes

_____
_____
_____
_____
_____
_____
_____

Chapter 3. Marketing Blueprints

4. Seven P's of the Marketing Mix

There are seven elements of the marketing mix that largely determine your success in business. A change in any one of these elements can change your level of sales, profitability, and results.

1. **Product/Service:** What exactly is your product or service? What does it do for your customer? How does it improve his or her life or work? What products or services are you going to offer? What products or services are you not going to offer? Any change in the products or services you offer can dramatically change the entire nature of your business.

    1. _____

    2. _____

    3. _____

2. **Price:** How much are you going to charge for your product? Will you sell wholesale or retail? If you give volume discounts for large purchases, how much will you charge at that time? How do your prices compare with those charged by your competitors? Are they higher or lower? How do you justify your prices? Any change to your pricing strategy can have a dramatic effect on your sales results and profits.

    1. _____

    2. _____

    3. _____

3. **Place:** Where exactly are you going to locate your business? Where are your customers? Do you sell from a retail storefront? Do you sell by telephone and Internet from your offices? A change in the location of your business activities—the place where you make contact with your customer, can change the nature of your business.

    1. _____

    2. _____

    3. _____

101

4. **Promotion:** How do you advertise and attract customers? Once you have attracted potential customers, what is the specific sales process that you use to convert those prospects into customers? What systems do you use for developing and maintaining a successful sales process to get customers to buy from you?

   1. _____

   2. _____

   3. _____

5. **Packaging:** What do your product, service, place of business, and every visual element of your company look like to your customers? Customers are extremely visual. They form their first impression about you and your company within four seconds of seeing you for the first time. Looking from the outside, is every part of the customer's visual experience with your company excellent in every way? Any change to the visual impact that your product or service makes on your prospect can have a dramatic effect on his or her behavior.

   1. _____

   2. _____

   3. _____

6. **Positioning:** How are you positioned in the minds and hearts of your customer? What words do your customers use when they talk about you and describe you to others? If your name were mentioned in a customer survey, how would customers and non-customers refer to you and your business? The way people think about you and talk about you when you are not there is a critical factor that largely determines whether they buy from you or recommend you to their friends.

   1. _____

   2. _____

   3. _____

Chapter 3. Marketing Blueprints

7. **People:** Who exactly are the people who interact with your customers? What do they look like? How do they dress? What do they say? What kinds of personality do they have? Prospective customers are largely emotional. They make most of their decisions based on the way they are treated by the people in your organization. What kind of "people experience" do customers have when they deal with you? How could you improve it?

1. _____

2. _____

3. _____

Notes

5. Finding a New Product or Service

New product development is an essential part of business, whether you are starting a business or you have been in business for some time. No matter how popular, your products and services become obsolescent over time and must be replaced by something better, faster, cheaper, or easier to use.

There are several ways to find new products and services. You should use as many of these methods as possible throughout your business career.

1. **Read everything you can find:** We've mentioned the adage, "Fish where the fish are." If you are looking for new products, services, or business opportunities, read the magazines and newspapers where they are offered. Read all the trade magazines in your field and in business in general. Read all the business magazines, newspapers, other publications, and even newsletters in your area of interest. Subscribe to everything that you can find. Don't be cheap or lazy in this area. List three publications you read, or are going to read, from now on.

    1. _____
    2. _____
    3. _____

2. **Attend trade shows, fairs, and exhibitions in your field:** In reading newspapers and magazines, you will learn about trade shows being held all over the country in your area of specialization. Currently, there are more than 5,000 trade shows every year. What trade shows could you attend?

    1. _____
    2. _____
    3. _____

3. **Read the business press:** Look for new product or service ideas that are being featured as news stories. Read *Forbes*, *Fortune*, and *BusinessWeek*. Read *The Wall Street Journal* and *Investor's Business Daily*. Read the business and business opportunity sections in your local newspaper. Be prepared to look at a lot

Chapter 3. Marketing Blueprints

of opportunities before you find the right one for you. What three news sources do you, or could you, read each day?

1. _____
2. _____
3. _____

4. **Keep your eyes open while you are traveling:** Many products or services are never sold outside of their home markets—local, national, or even in other countries. Many people have become wealthy by seeing a product for sale while traveling overseas, inquiring and getting the rights to distribute it exclusively in the United States or in their market area, and starting a successful business as a result. Where could you visit to find new business ideas?

1. _____
2. _____
3. _____

5. **Study demographic trends:** In his book *Innovation and Entrepreneurship*, Peter Drucker says that one of the major sources of new product and service ideas is demographic trends. Akio Morita, co-founder of Sony, discovered a new product in this way. His children and grandchildren were continually playing boom boxes around the house, seemingly unable to go anywhere without listening to their loud music. Morita, in a fit of exasperation, began wondering if it was possible to develop a technology that would enable people to listen to their music without disturbing others around them. He came up with the idea for the Sony Walkman, which went on to achieve sales of more than a billion dollars. List three trends that will create demand for new products and services.

1. _____
2. _____
3. _____

6. **Look into your own field or skills:** Look under your own feet. Remember the "Acres of Diamonds" concept, which says that what you are looking for may be right under your own feet. It may be within your own knowledge, education, experience, interest, or current job. There may be a million-dollar idea staring you right in the face. List three of your talents, skills, or talents that might you contain a business idea for you:

   1. _____

   2. _____

   3. _____

List three ways that you could use to find new products or services:

   1. _____

   2. _____

   3. _____

Notes

_____
_____
_____
_____
_____
_____
_____
_____
_____
_____

Chapter 3. Marketing Blueprints

6. How to Do Fast, Cheap Market Research

Before launching a product or service or any new business venture, considerable time must be spent in research. The payoff will be in excess of 10:1 in the time and money saved or earned.

1. **Find out every detail of the product or service.** Make yourself an expert. Go onto the Internet and Google the product or service. Explore every source of information on it. Imagine that you are going to be grilled by venture capitalists or bankers and you must be able to demonstrate a thorough knowledge of the product or service.

2. **Read all the trade magazines, articles, and stories on the business, industry or service.** Sometimes one observation in a current publication can be critical to business success or failure.

3. **Seek out people in the same business and ask their opinion of the product or service.** If you are thinking of buying a business, talk with everyone who is in that business and ask them what they think. Would they get into the business again if they were starting over today? What advice or counsel would they give someone who was interested in getting into this business?

You will be amazed at how open and helpful people are when you ask for their advice. They are not secretive at all. And sometimes they can open your eyes to possibilities or pitfalls that you would never have seen on your own.

Take your product or service to your bank manager (whether you have a company account or a personal checking or savings account) for his or her opinion or advice. Your bank manager is talking to businesspeople with ideas for new products and services every day. Often, he or she will have observations or even internal banking publications that can give you ideas and insights that are priceless. Don't be afraid to ask.

4. **Ask your family, friends, and acquaintances for information, ideas, and opinions.** Especially, listen to the women in your life. They are the best shoppers around and they now make or control the majority of buying decisions in America.

When you take your product or service to a woman, she will give you an immediate, honest, accurate, and intuitive answer about its attractiveness and marketability. In addition, most women know a lot about what else is available and how to compare your product or service with alternatives. If a woman is negative about your product or service idea, you should immediately pull back and see if it is possible to modify it to make it more attractive.

5. **Visit prospective customers for the product or service and ask if they would buy it.** Prospective customers are an extraordinarily good source of market information. If you ask them their opinion of your product or service, they will tell you immediately—and they are almost always accurate. They will not hold back. They will give you insights and feedback that you could not get by hiring a market research firm to poll hundreds or thousands of people.

6. **Investigate all competitors for the product or service.** Who else is offering a competitive product? What are the special features or benefits of that product or service? And, especially, why would someone switch to buy from you?

Chapter 3. Marketing Blueprints

7. Nine Great Marketing Questions

There is a single marketing question you can ask at every stage of your business:

What exactly is to be sold, and **to whom** is it to be sold, and **how** is it going to be marketed, advertised, and sold, and **by whom**, and at **what** price and terms, and **how** is it to be manufactured, produced, and delivered, and **how**, and **by whom**, and under **what** conditions, and **how** is it to be serviced to ensure complete customer satisfaction leading to resales and referrals?

This is the great business question, which must be broken down into nine smaller questions.

1. **What is to be sold?** You must answer this question in terms of what it does for your customer, how it benefits him or her, what problems it solves, and the specific improvement that it brings about in your customer's life or work.

    1. _____

    2. _____

    3. _____

2. **To whom is it to be sold?** Who is your customer, exactly? What are his or her age, education, income, family status, job, occupation, and industry? Where do your customers live, when do they buy, what else are they buying today, and why would they buy from you?

    1. _____

    2. _____

    3. _____

3. **How is it to be sold?** You must determine the exact sales process, from the first customer contact—whether face to face, on the Internet, or on the telephone—and the exact words that will be used, step by step, to identify customer needs, present the product or service as a solution to their needs, answer objections, close the sale, and get the customer to commit to the purchase.

    1. _____

    2. _____

    3. _____

Way to Wealth Workbook: Blueprints for Business Success

4. **By whom is it to be sold?** You must be clear about the individuals who will be responsible for the direct contact and sales activities, for converting a prospect attracted by your advertising into a customer. The failure to clearly identify and train your salespeople is a major reason for business underachievement and failure.

   1. _____

   2. _____

   3. _____

5. **What marketing, advertising, and promotional activities will you use?** How will you generate leads and attract prospective customers? What media will you use to advertise and promote your product or service? How much will it cost? How effective will it be? How many leads do you expect to generate for the amount of money that you intend to spend for that purpose? How will you position your product or service against competitive products or services to get people to call or come to you rather than to go to them?

   1. _____

   2. _____

   3. _____

6. **How much will you charge?** Exactly what will your prices be, not only for an individual sale, but also for volume sales, wholesale, discount sales, and sales in combination with other products or services? Determining the proper prices for your products or services is an art and a science and it can be critical to your success.

   1. _____

   2. _____

   3. _____

7. **How is the product to be produced, manufactured, and delivered to your customer?** What will it cost and how long will it take to produce the product or service? How much will you have to invest, how much money will you have tied up in inventory before you make the first sale and generate revenues? In

Chapter 3. Marketing Blueprints

what way will you deliver the product or service to your customer in a satisfactory form so that he or she is happy with it?

1. _____
2. _____
3. _____

8. **How will the product be paid for?** What prices and terms will you offer? Will you require full payment in advance or part payment or will you offer 30-, 60-, 90-day terms of purchase? What are the standards in your industry? What sort of prices and terms will you have to offer to get the business? How could you revise these prices and terms to make them more satisfactory to yourself and your business?

    1. _____
    2. _____
    3. _____

9. **How will you service the customer after the purchase?** What steps will you take to make sure that your customer is so satisfied that he or she will buy again and refer you to others? Your customer service policy is the linchpin of your business. You can succeed only to the degree to which people are satisfied to such an extent that they buy again and tell their friends.

    1. _____
    2. _____
    3. _____

You should think through the answers to these questions. Each time you have a slowdown or difficulty in sales, you should revisit these questions to make sure that your answers are accurate and acceptable to your prospective customer market.

8. Seven Reasons Why People Buy Things

There are **seven critical categories** that determine purchase decisions, in descending order of importance. Your job is to continually analyze your business, your products, and your services, and compare them against these buying motivations.

You may have the best product, but if you're trying to sell it by appealing to the wrong emotion, customers will ignore it. Many of the great business breakthroughs have been the result of repositioning the product or service so that it appealed to the same customer, but in a different way.

1. **Emotions:** The feeling or experience the customer expects to enjoy by buying, owning, and using your product or service. What particular emotions does your product or service trigger in your customer?

    1. _____
    2. _____
    3. _____

2. **Improvement:** The impact of your product or service on the customer and his or her work life. How does your product or service improve the life and work of your customer?

    1. _____
    2. _____
    3. _____

3. **Performance:** How your product or service works. What does your product or service do to provide the benefit or satisfaction your customer expects?

    1. _____
    2. _____
    3. _____

Chapter 3. Marketing Blueprints

4. **Result or benefit:** The tangible event or condition that comes about from using your product or service. What is the specific result or benefit your customer receives from your product or service?

    1. _____
    2. _____
    3. _____

5. **Special attribute:** The particular quality that your customer remembers, often your "unique selling proposition." What special qualities of your product or company does your customer remember most?

    1. _____
    2. _____
    3. _____

6. **Comparisons:** The way you position your product or service against competitive products or services. In what three ways is your product or service superior to your competitors'?

    1. _____
    2. _____
    3. _____

7. **Price:** The meaning of the *cost relative to the cost of other products or services* or other uses of the same amount of money. In what ways are your prices better than those of your competitors?

    1. _____
    2. _____
    3. _____

9. Key Concerns in Making a Buying Decision

Each customer strives to satisfy different combinations of needs, wants, and desires in every purchase decision. The greater clarity you have regarding the mind and emotions of your potential customer, the easier it is for you to advertise, promote, and attract people who will buy from you rather than from your competitors.

1. **Personal:** Emotions, aesthetics, the feeling the customer expects from buying. How will your customer feel as the result of buying your product or service?

    1. _____
    2. _____
    3. _____

2. **Utility:** Operation. Does the product or service work, do the job, improve your customer's life? What specific functions does your product or service perform?

    1. _____
    2. _____
    3. _____

3. **Convenience:** How easy is it to use and benefit from your product or service? In what ways is it easier for your customer to benefit from your product or service than from those of your competitors?

    1. _____
    2. _____
    3. _____

4. **Functionality:** How does it fit? Work in practice? How does it bring about the results or benefits you promise?

    1. _____
    2. _____
    3. _____

Chapter 3. Marketing Blueprints

5. **Result:** Tangible event or condition that comes about from using your product. What result does your customer get from buying and using your product or service?

   1. _____
   2. _____
   3. _____

6. **Attribute:** Positioning, brand, the particular quality your customer remembers. What are the most important qualities of your product or service that your customer remembers?

   1. _____
   2. _____
   3. _____

7. **Comparative:** The way your product or service is positioned against competitors. In what ways is your product or service superior to those of your competitors?

   1. _____
   2. _____
   3. _____

Notes

_____
_____
_____
_____
_____
_____
_____

10. Becoming the Quality Choice

In every business or industry, the top 20% of companies earn 80% of the profits. For this reason, thousands of companies have been studied for many years in an attempt to determine the specific factors that lead to greater growth and prosperity, as opposed to average growth or even decline or bankruptcy.

One of the most important discoveries of the PIMS Study at Harvard, covering 620 companies over a 20-year period, was that the perceived level of quality of a company's products and services was the critical factor in determining its sales, growth, and profitability.

For example, if a customer survey were conducted in your community and customers were asked to rate all the companies in your industry on a scale of one to ten, the company that customers rated the highest would also turn out, on examination of its financial statements, to be the most profitable in that industry.

Each Segment Has Quality Leaders

Each market and each product or service in a market can be divided into segments. These segments refer to the products or services and to the types of customers who purchase these products or services. Because of this segmentation, it is possible for a company that sells a low-priced product to achieve the highest quality ranking in a particular market segment.

The jeweler Tiffany & Co. sells high-priced jewelry and other products primarily to wealthy people for whom price is not a concern. Among quality jewelers, Tiffany has an extremely high quality ranking and is, by extension, very profitable.

Zales jewelers is a national chain that sells to middle-class people. It has a wide selection of engagement rings, wedding rings, and other jewelry that family members and friends buy for each other. In their market segment, Zales has a high quality ranking in serving its particular type of customers and has therefore been highly profitable year after year.

McDonald's can certainly not be compared to a first-class restaurant, but in its market segment McDonald's is famous for excellent-quality fast food. This is why the company is so successful and profitable in the fast-food market and why McDonald's is so profitable.

Chapter 3. Marketing Blueprints

Determine Your Own Quality Ranking

If you were to survey people in your market to determine the quality ranking of your company, how would you rank? First? That would be nice—but this may not be true at the moment. _____

_____

What is most important is that you determine your relative quality ranking at the current time. Let us say that, out of ten companies in your business that sell to much the same customers, your quality ranking is sixth. If you could examine the financial statements of your competitors, you would find that your level of profitability is probably also sixth in your market.

Move up One Rank

Your goal now is not necessarily to attempt to be first in your market. That would probably be too much of a leap. Your goal is to improve your quality ranking by one level, to move from sixth to fifth, for example. You can do this—and within the foreseeable future.

What would you have to do, starting today, to improve the way customers think about you and talk about you when your name comes up or when they describe you to other people? What should you do first? What should you do second? What would be your plan to improve your quality ranking?

1. _____

2. _____

3. _____

Your ultimate goal is to be in the top 10% in your industry and, ideally, to be the best. For you to move your company up one quality ranking, you must know exactly why other companies rank ahead of you. One of the best ways to find this out is to ask your non-customers why they prefer to buy from your competitors rather than from you. What value do they perceive? What differences do they see between your business and your competitors?

1. _____

2. _____

3. _____

Instead of being defensive or dismissive, be curious and open. Ask questions and listen carefully until you know exactly what your customer considers value that you are not currently offering.

Resolve to Be the Best

Every company needs values, vision, purpose, and mission. Everyone in every company needs something to aspire to. And there is nothing more motivational or inspirational in a company than the commitment by the business owner to ultimately be the best in the industry.

There is nothing that will attract better people and bring better work out of the people in your company than a wholehearted determination on your part to get better and better in what you do until your customers ultimately rank you as "the best in the business."

Your Most Valuable Asset

According to a Harvard University study, the most valuable asset that a company has is its *reputation*. This is best defined as "how you are known to your customers."

Because the credibility of your advertising and your offerings is the critical determinant of whether people buy from you, your reputation is more important than any other single factor.

The most powerful form of advertising in our society is word-of-mouth advertising. This takes place when your satisfied customers tell your prospective customers how good you are and how much they enjoy doing business with you.

Word-of-mouth advertising is free. It comes when you provide excellent products and services to your customers and then take care of your customers with excellent follow-up service. You must do this consistently.

Customers are generally reluctant to tell their friends and associates to patronize a particular business because they're afraid. They worry that if they recommend a product or service to someone, that person will be disappointed if he or she does not get what assured and expected.

Give Excellent Customer Service

For this reason, the highest and best form of promotion is for you to take wonderful care of your customers, every single time. It will take you a long time to build a reputation for excellent customer service, but once you have established it, it can help you to attract more and better business than anything else you can do.

Chapter 3. Marketing Blueprints

There are some companies that are extremely successful, but they do very little advertising. Instead, they focus all of their efforts on taking such great care of their customers that these customers not only return and buy again, but they tell everyone else how good the business is.

It is estimated that a happy customer will tell five to eight other prospective customers about a product or service. On the other hand, an unhappy customer will tell ten to 15 people not to buy that product or service. In addition, because of the Internet, a happy or unhappy customer can tell thousands of people about his or her experience with you.

Notes

WAY TO WEALTH WORKBOOK: BLUEPRINTS FOR BUSINESS SUCCESS

11. Buying Customers—Determining Your Costs of Acquisition

One of the most important jobs you do is to buy customers at a cost that is lower than the profit you earn from sales to that customer. The whole purpose of advertising, promotion, discounts, and special offers or bonuses is to buy customers in some way.

You must be clear about how much you can spend per customer or you will lose money when you advertise and promote.

You determine how much you can spend by conducting the following analysis:

1. Determine your average sale. _____

2. Determine your net profit per sale. _____

3. Your net profit per sale is the maximum you can pay to acquire a customer the first time. _____

4. Determine the exact cost of the advertisement or promotion. _____

5. Divide your net profit number into the cost of the advertising to determine how many units you will have to sell to justify advertising this way. _____

6. Double the number of sales that you must get to determine the minimum number of sales necessary to justify this advertising. _____

7. Advertise only if you are confident that you will earn a 100% return or more on your investment.

    Example: Your product sells for $100
    Your profit per item is $30
    The advertisement costs $3,000
    Divide ad costs by profit per item = 100 units
    Multiply number of units by 2 = 200 units

   You must be able to sell 200 units to justify the advertisement.

Chapter 3. Marketing Blueprints

12. Lifetime Value of a Customer

One of your most important calculations in business is the lifetime value of each customer, on average, in terms of sales and profitability.

You can actually lose money on the first sale, or break even, if you can be confident that the customer will buy from you several times.

Some companies actually give the product away and lose money to acquire the customer for the first time, as long as they are confident that the customer will buy again.

What is the lifetime value of your customers? How often does a satisfied customer buy from you, and how much profit do you make each time?

The cost of acquisition of each customer is the key number in determining all your advertising, promotion and sales activities

How much does your average customer buy from you, and how much can you invest to attract more customers like this?

1. _____
2. _____
3. _____

Notes

13. How to Write Effective Advertising

There are several keys to writing effective advertising. The first is to focus on a single product, service or benefit. Always imagine that a child is going to read your advertisement and then turn to another child and tell that other child what you sell and why someone should buy it from you.

Make your advertising simple, clear and direct. Focus on a single reason why people should respond to the advertisement, rather than responding to the hundreds of other advertisements that they see and hear every day.

Focus on What Your Product or Service Does

Here is an unhappy little secret of business. I can't repeat it often enough. No one likes to admit it, but here it is: Nobody cares about what your product or service *is*. Nobody cares what your product or service is. Customers care only about what your product or service *does* for them. Customers care only about how your product or service *improves* their life or work.

There are lists of reasons and motivations that cause people to buy. But you can boil them down into one single buying motivation: "improvement"!

Customers buy improvement—morning, noon, and night. They are concerned only about whether your product or service will improve their life or work in a particular way, right now. When you write an advertisement of any kind, the focal point must be the improvement you offer. And you must make it clear.

Call for Immediate Action

The second key to writing effective advertising is to tell the prospect exactly what action you want him or her to take immediately. For example, "Come in today before 9:00 p.m. while supplies last!"

Here is an important rule: make it *easy* for your customer to buy from you. Be sure that your call to action is simple and easy to follow, especially on radio, where listeners generally cannot take notes. Keep numbers to a minimum; they confuse prospective customers.

Here is another rule: do not try to *create a need* in your advertising. Only address a need that the customer has already. Address a pain that the customer is feeling already and wants to have relieved. Address a lack that the customer experiences already. Offer to provide a benefit that the customer desires already. Your goal is to use your advertising to talk to customers who already want what you are selling. The purpose of your advertising is to get the already-qualified customer to buy from you, rather than from someone else, and to buy now.

Chapter 3. Marketing Blueprints

The Three-Part Formula for Effective Advertising

There is a formula for writing effective advertising, especially for radio and television.

First, you describe the problem the customer wants to solve, the need the customer wants to satisfy, or the pain the customer wants to relieve. This immediately grabs the attention of your ideal prospect.

Second, you describe the solution. You describe the ideal way to solve the problem, satisfy the need, or relieve the pain. This triggers buying desire in the prospect's mind.

Third, you describe your product or service as the best solution available and end the advertisement with a call to action. You tell the prospect to visit your place of business or to phone to set up an appointment. You tell the customer to visit your Web site or take some action to acquire the product or service immediately. This offers the customer an immediate way to get the solution or benefit he or she desires now.

Write Your Own Advertising

Here is a simple example:

> Drivers have serious car accidents every day when their worn tires give out in fast freeway traffic (problem/pain). Enjoy the peace of mind and security of knowing that you are driving on brand new tires (solution). ABC Tire Company offers you great prices, quick service, and skilled technicians (best solution). Come in today at 425 Western Avenue or phone 619 555-5555 (call to action). Don't wait. Do it today. Come to 425 Western Avenue or phone us to set up an appointment at 619 555-5555. You will be glad you did.

You don't need to be an advertising genius to write effective copy. You simply have to focus clearly on the *most* important benefit you offer. Make it clear what your product or service does to improve the customer's life or work and tell the customer what action he or she should take immediately to acquire your product or service.

Direct Response Advertising

You must treat all advertising for your business as direct response advertising. This means that your advertising must trigger immediate responses from prospective customers. Your message must translate into immediate sales—today.

Creative advertising sells! Period. Effective advertising sells! Period. If it doesn't trigger immediate responses, discontinue it immediately.

The easiest way to test your advertising is to run it up the flagpole and see if anyone salutes. The easiest way to measure the success of your advertisement is that you attract immediate responses that convert into customers who buy more of your product or service and yield profits greater than the cost of the advertising.

Practice Makes Perfect

If you keep testing and measuring, practicing trial and error, asking your customers for information on how they heard about you and what caused them to contact you, you can eventually develop a method for advertising that pays for itself every time. Once you have developed the ability to attract customers profitably, you can advertise more and grow your business almost without limit.

One final point about marketing, advertising, sales, and customer service: always remember to tune into the customers' favorite radio station, WII-FM, which means "What's in It for Me?"

In the final analysis, customers are selfish and expedient. They have a thousand choices. They buy a product or service only when they are convinced that it is the ideal choice for them, at this time, at this price, in this location, and that there is nothing better available as an alternative. Every advertisement should make this clear.

Notes

Chapter 3. Marketing Blueprints

14. 24 Ways to Sell Your Product or Service

There are many different ways to sell a product or service in this country. The average business uses only one or two of these methods. Fortunately, the more of these methods with which you are familiar and experiment on a limited scale, the more likely you are to pinpoint a formula for sales success that will make you wealthy.

1. **Personal Sales:** Personal direct selling is the best of all sales methods. This is something that you are doing, one way or another; from the first day you start in business. You are selling your product or service. You are selling your ideas. You are selling yourself and your leadership. You are selling your abilities to pay your suppliers, your backers, and your bankers. You are selling your authority to your staff. You are selling continually. Lists three ways to increase your personal sales:

    1. _____
    2. _____
    3. _____

2. **Retail Sales:** The second way to sell a product is through retail sales. You can sell your products through your own store or through wholesalers or retailers. Many tens of thousands of products are designed, developed, manufactured, and sold through wholesalers and retailers. This is perhaps the largest single method of sales in the world. How could you increase or create retail sales?

    1. _____
    2. _____
    3. _____

3. **Distributors:** You can recruit distributors for your product in market areas beyond the one where you do business. Selling through a distributorship can be as *simple* as giving an individual or company the exclusive or non-exclusive right to sell your products in its area or to its current customers.

    Setting up distributorships can be as *complex* as selecting the right people and companies, training them thoroughly to sell and deliver your product or service, supplying them with all the products and materials they need to conduct their business, and supporting them 24/7 to ensure that they are successful in selling your products.

WAY TO WEALTH WORKBOOK: BLUEPRINTS FOR BUSINESS SUCCESS

Distributors are invariably independent businesses with their own names and identities—and their own ideas about how to conduct their businesses. Aside from getting them to agree to certain performance standards and working as closely with them as they will allow, you have little control over how they operate. Nonetheless, setting up distributors for your products or services can enable you to expand nationally and internationally in a short time. How could you get distributors for your product or service?

1. _____

2. _____

3. _____

4. **Newspapers:** Another way to sell a product is through the newspaper. The purpose of newspaper advertising is to generate direct and immediate responses that translate into sales and profits greatly in excess of the cost of advertising. All newspapers advertising is aimed at getting people to take action *now*. It is aimed at getting them to phone you and buy or to come into your store so that you can present your products and sell to them immediately. What are three ways you could use newspapers to increase your sales?

   1. _____

   2. _____

   3. _____

Is it paying for itself? A marketing consultant who worked for me many years ago had a simple formula, "Creative advertising sells!" He said that immediate responses and sales results were the only measure of whether or not the advertising was any good.

Some years ago, I was promoting a product with radio and newspaper advertising that had been written by an agency that was apparently not very good at what it did. One day, in the midst of this advertising campaign, another advertising executive, representing his own advertising agency, phoned me and asked me how sales were going. A bit embarrassed, I told him that sales were going fine. He said, "I have only one question for you: Is your phone ringing?"

As it happened, in spite of many thousands of dollars of advertising, the phone was not ringing at all. I invited him in to make me a new proposal for a different approach to our advertising. His ideas were excellent. We accepted them and within one week, the new ads were causing our phones to ring off the hook. I always apply that same rule to the advertising of my clients, "Is your phone

Chapter 3. Marketing Blueprints

ringing?" If it's not, change your advertising immediately. How can you get your phone to ring?

1. _____

2. _____

3. _____

5. **Direct Mail:** You can sell your product or service through direct mail. Direct mail allows you to pinpoint your market and aim your promotions at those people who would be the most likely to buy within the shortest time.

   Successful direct mail depends on your ability to acquire a good mailing list and offering a product or service selected for that specific group of customers. Direct mail allows you to focus on doctors, dentists, lawyers, sports car owners, seminar attendees, or any other demographic group that you can identify.

   There are several organizations throughout the country that develop and supply mailing lists for direct mail marketing. Dun & Bradstreet has been a market leader in this area for many years. USA Direct of Omaha has names, addresses, and data for more than 100 million people, in every category, throughout the United States. There are mailing list brokers in the Yellow Pages in virtually every major city. You can also find all the information you need regarding mailing lists on the Internet.

   The number, sophistication, and quality of mailing lists available today are remarkable. The more specific you can be about the best type of prospect for what you are selling, the more precisely your mailing list can be designed and the more effective your direct mailing campaign will be. How could you sell with direct mail?

   1. _____

   2. _____

   3. _____

6. **Mail Order:** Another way to sell is through mail order. You can place ads in publications that appeal to your particular customer group. Entrepreneur Paul Hawkins built a $45-million business selling garden tools by running small ads in magazines that were read by people who garden as a hobby. Other people get started in business by contracting for products at wholesale and then selling

them at retail in the classified sections of magazines and newspapers. How could you use mail order to sell your products or services?

1. _____

2. _____

3. _____

7. **The Internet:** You can market your product or service through the Internet. You can set up a Web site, offer specialized products and services to a particular type of customer, and then work in cooperation with businesses that use their Web sites to appeal to that same type of customer. How could sell more of your products on the Internet?

1. _____

2. _____

3. _____

The era of spam marketing through the Internet is coming to an end through government regulation. For the foreseeable future you will sell on the Internet by offering free information in a specialized area and making your offer widely known. When customers come to your site to take advantage of your free offer, you can then sell them high-quality products and services, backed by an unconditional guarantee. As you develop an expanding network of happy customers, they will tell others about your site and your customer list will start to grow.

There are many misunderstandings about the Internet. Some people suggest that it is easy to start an Internet business and make a lot of money. The fact is that it is not easy to start any business and make a lot of money. Every business requires a tremendous amount of thoughtful planning and preparation before you begin. It then takes a good deal of time to build your business, one sale at a time.

Almost all products sold on the Internet are clear and specific. The customers know exactly what they are looking for when they use the Internet. It is almost impossible to create a demand for a new product on the Internet, because it is impossible to touch, taste, feel or experiment with it.

The most successful Internet businesses are those that sell known products at competitive prices with unconditional guarantees. Think about Amazon.com or

Chapter 3. Marketing Blueprints

BarnesandNoble.com as well as travel sites such as Expedia.com and Priceline.com. What Internet sites could you use to sell your products or services?

1. _____

2. _____

3. _____

8. **Direct Selling:** You can sell your products and services directly, from office to office or door to door. This form of selling requires an ability to write or telephone to set up appointments, to visit the prospect personally, to identify the prospect's needs, and to make an effective sales presentation.

   Often direct selling requires "cold calling." This means that you have to phone or visit people whom you have never seen or met. In cold calling, the rejection rate is high. You need to be tough and persistent. However, once you learn that rejection is not personal and you conquer your fear of cold calling, you can start and build successful sales in virtually any market. How could you use direct selling to sell more of your product?

   1. _____

   2. _____

   3. _____

9. **Seminar Selling:** You can advertise to bring together prospective customers who are interested in your product or service for a group presentation. During this presentation, you can explain what you offer, explain why it's an ideal product or service for those in the audience, and encourage the seminar attendees to buy what you are selling or arrange for a private meeting later.

   Seminar selling is used primarily to sell business seminars and services and financial advice and planning. The key to success in this method of selling is to give excellent value and instruction on your subject to demonstrate your expertise and to create a desire to learn more. This way of selling can be successful if you can attract a large enough group of qualified prospects, usually via newspaper, direct mail, and radio. How can you use seminar selling to sell more of your product or service?

   1. _____

   2. _____

   3. _____

10. **Party Plan:** You can sell your products through what is called a "party plan." Some merchandise—such as Tupperware, beauty products, specialty foods, and certain clothing lines—can be sold in homes. The salesperson invites friends over for a presentation, demonstrates and sells the products to those in attendance, and then receives a premium or commission on all sales. Hundreds of millions of dollars of merchandise are sold on the party plan system every year. How might you use the party plan to sell your products or services?

    1. _____
    2. _____
    3. _____

11. **Co-op Mailings:** You can sell your product or service through co-op mailings. Many large mailing firms or other companies will include your product flyer or product brochure with their mailings or invoices in exchange for a share of your gross sales.

    If you have an American Express, MasterCard, or Visa card, you are familiar with the special offers that come with each invoice. These companies send out information on dozens of products throughout the year along with their invoices.

    One of the great advantages to co-op mailings is that there is no cost to you, except for printing the promotional material, until the sales are generated. How could you use co-op mailings to seel more of your product or service?

    1. _____
    2. _____
    3. _____

12. **The Government:** You can sell your product or services to governments at all levels—city, county, state, and federal. The government is the biggest single customer in the country, consuming hundreds of billions of dollars worth of products and services each year. You can make a fortune by finding a product that government organizations need and want at a particular time.

    If you have a product or service that can be used by government agencies, you should approach city, county, state, and federal government offices. Find out everything you can about how to sell to government officials. Find out how to get onto their bidding lists. Find out who does the purchasing and the purposes and criteria. Sometimes, you can even develop a product specifically for various

Chapter 3. Marketing Blueprints

governments or for a specific government department, such as the U.S. Department of Defense. What government agencies or departments could your product or service be ideal for?

1. _____

2. _____

3. _____

13. **Manufacturers' Representatives:** You can sell your product through manufacturers' representatives. There are companies throughout the country that represent a variety of products in a specific market area. Often, they will specialize in selling to a particular type of customer or in carrying a particular type of product line.

    You can advertise for manufacturers' representatives to work for you on commission in other market areas. Advertise in the specific magazines and publications that they read. The best part is that you pay them straight commission: there is no cost to you unless they make a sale. What manufacturer's representatives are there who could carry your product or service?

    1. _____

    2. _____

    3. _____

14. **Chain Stores:** You can sell your product through chain stores. Sometimes chain stores have hundreds of outlets nationwide. You only need to sell your product to one person, to one buyer at the head office, and it will go into hundreds of stores.

    Many entrepreneurs have made their fortunes by getting a company like Wal-Mart, Target, or Kmart to carry their product in all its outlets. Even though these big buyers will squeeze the entrepreneurs down to the last penny, the volume of sales can still make selling through these large chain stores extremely profitable. What chain stores could carry your product?

    1. _____

    2. _____

    3. _____

15. **Discount Stores:** You can sell through discount stores. They prefer to carry products at prices below the normal retail prices. Sometimes you can repackage or even relabel your product to sell through discount stores so that your discount sales won't hurt your sales at full retail prices. What might you do to sell your products through discount stores?

    1. _____

    2. _____

    3. _____

16. **Supermarkets:** You can sell through supermarkets. These chains often carry a large number of non-food items. If one chain of supermarkets will carry your product and it is appropriate for their type of customer, you could sell an enormous amount in a short time. What opportunities are there for you to sell your product through supermarkets?

    1. _____

    2. _____

    3. _____

17. **Department Stores:** You can sell through department stores. Their product buyers are very astute, and if they like your product, the stores can become major customers for you.

    One of the most important things to do, before you begin producing or importing a particular product or service, is to visit product buyers at these stores and get their opinions. These people deal with vendors all day long and usually have excellent instincts for what will sell in the current market. They are not always correct, but their input can save you a lot of time and money. What department stores could carry your product?

    1. _____

    2. _____

    3. _____

18. **Wholesalers:** You can sell through wholesalers. Wholesalers will often carry your products along with the other lines that they sell directly to retailers.

    If you use wholesalers, you will have to sell to them at well below retail prices. Their primary concern will be the profit margin they can earn between what

Chapter 3. Marketing Blueprints

they pay you for your product and what they can charge their retail customers. As a result, they will push hard to squeeze your prices down as low as possible.

Here is an important point. Whenever you are selling to wholesalers, retailers, discount stores, department stores, chain stores, or grocery stores, they will all have one measure in common. Their primary concern is turnover. How quickly will the product sell and how much profit will they make per unit? Sometimes this is known as "velocity." What will be the speed of turnover multiplied by the amount of money they can make from selling these items?

These people are not interested in prestige, status, attractiveness, or appealing to a narrow market segment. They care about the profit—the volume of sales multiplied by the profit per item. When you talk with them, the quality of your product will be of some concern to them but the profitability of carrying your product will be all-important. Be sure to appeal to this main interest in everything you do and say. How might you demonstrate the profitability of your product to wholesalers?

1. _____
2. _____
3. _____

19. **Premium Sales:** You can sell your product as a premium. Companies may purchase your products to give away as prizes, awards, or bonuses for purchasing something else. If your product is inexpensive enough and the perceived value is high enough, companies could be interested in buying it and giving it away as a low-cost incentive to get people to purchase their product or service.

    Look for companies that use prizes, awards, and bonuses to get new business. Sometimes these companies can buy your product in large quantities. If a company wants to give away a large number of them, you can privately label your product. What are three companies that could give your product away as a gift?

    1. _____
    2. _____
    3. _____

20. **Advertising Specialty:** You can sell your product as an advertising specialty. Companies may purchase your product to imprint with their name and give it away as gifts and incentives to their customers. Some popular advertising specialties are embossed pens, calendars, flying discs (e.g., Frisbee®), or baseball

133

caps. Often, companies will give away pocket calendars, radios, and even small computers as advertising specialties. What companies could sell yor product as an advertising specialty?

1. _____

2. _____

3. _____

21. **Franchising:** You can sell your product in large quantities through franchising. Many businesses have the capacity to be franchised and be rolled out to other areas. Franchise businesses now account for many billions of dollars in retail sales, throughout the United States and throughout the world.

    A franchise is a proven success system. It is a business system from which all the bugs and defects have been removed. It is a profit-making system that can work for anybody, virtually anywhere, if he or she follows the business system exactly the way it has been designed.

    Once you have developed a successful business system, such as McDonald's, FedEx Kinko's, or Krispy Kreme Doughnuts, you have a model that is replicable. Like a recipe, it can be duplicated over and over, getting the same results for each new franchise.

    McDonald's has more than 30,000 franchises worldwide. Because the McDonald's franchise system has been tested and proven so many thousands of time, in every type of market, there have been only one or two McDonald's franchise failures in history.

    A Proven System. With a good franchise, the sellers of the franchise can predict with some accuracy how much the owner will earn each year as the result of following the system.

    But franchising requires that you develop a successful system first. Franchising requires that you develop a profitable business that can be copied. It is amazing how many people come up with a business idea and begin thinking about franchising it before they have even made it successful. The fact is that the average company that franchises does not do so until it has have been in business for eight to ten years. Most companies never franchise at all. If you are considering buying a franchise, investigate before you invest and look for a track record of success. What are three things you could do to turn your business into a franchise?

    1. _____

    2. _____

    3. _____

Chapter 3. Marketing Blueprints

22. **Trade Shows:** You can sell your product through trade shows. Buyers from thousand of companies attend trade shows every year to find new products to offer to their customers. They know that the cutting edge of new product development is represented in trade shows and that one new product, at the right time, can earn millions of dollars.

    As I mentioned earlier, there are more than 5,000 trade shows each year. Many companies develop their entire business around their appearances in trade shows. List three trade shows you should be attending every year.

    1. _____

    2. _____

    3. _____

23. **Displays and Exhibits:** You can move your product to the market through shows, fairs, expositions, or even exhibits at conventions and fund-raising shows. High traffic count can result in big sales. Look for places where you can appear and display your product where a lot of potential buyers will be walking past. You want to be continually seeking ways to put your product in front of as many potential customers as possible. What shows or exhibits should you be in to sell more of your products?

    1. _____

    2. _____

    3. _____

24. **Fund-Raisers:** You can market your product through charities and fund-raisers. You can often sell your product through organizations that will sell it to raise funds. You can do this through churches, charitable organizations, the Chamber of Commerce, or schools. You can sell candy, nuts, toys, and items for schools, bands, and other fundraising organizations. List three ways you could use fund-raisers to increase your sales.

    1. _____

    2. _____

    3. _____

Most of these 24 ideas require energy and imagination more than money and risk. In many cases, you can take orders for the product before you place your orders with the manufacturer, thereby keeping your exposure limited until you develop a steady volume of sales.

CHAPTER FOUR

Sales Blueprints

In this chapter:

1. Sales Skills Assessment	138
2. Sales Planning Process	142
3. Seven Ways of Selling	145
4. Seven Qualities of Top Salespeople	150
5. Seven Best Sales-Closing Techniques	151
6. Four Levels of Customer Service	152
7. Seven Keys to Effective Networking	154
8. Seven Questions to Set Priorities in Selling	155

WAY TO WEALTH WORKBOOK: BLUEPRINTS FOR BUSINESS SUCCESS

1. Sales Skills Assessment

Why are some salespeople more successful than others?

Why do some salespeople sell and earn twice as much, five times, even ten times as much as others?

The difference is always *knowledge* and *skill!* The top salespeople are better at selling than the average salespeople.

Fortunately, all sales skills are l*earnable.* You can learn any skill you need to achieve any sales goal you set for yourself. In fact, you are probably only *one skill away* from **doubling** your income!

Ten key result areas of selling are described below. Give yourself a grade of 1-10 for each. This will help you to understand your strengths and weaknesses and what you can do to rapidly increase your sales and your income.

Successful selling is possible only when you become competent in the following areas. How are you doing? How true are these statements for you?

1. **Prospecting:** You have a steady stream of qualified prospects who take up most of your selling time.

    a. 80% of your time is spent with pre-qualified prospects.
    b. You have a proven system of developing new prospects.

    | **Grade:** | 1 | 2 | 3 | 4 | 5 | 6 | 7 | 8 | 9 | 10 |

2. **Building Rapport and Trust:** You have a pleasant, positive personality and easily make friends with prospects and customers.

    a. You genuinely like people and they like you.
    b. Your prospects and customers trust you and believe you and are happy to see you again.

    | **Grade:** | 1 | 2 | 3 | 4 | 5 | 6 | 7 | 8 | 9 | 10 |

3. **Identifying Needs:** You have an organized series of questions to accurately determine the needs of your prospect regarding your product or service.

    a. You conduct an effective needs analysis with each prospect.
    b. After your needs analysis, you and your prospect are clear about what he or she needs, the budget and the timing for purchase, and the major objections to be addressed.

    | **Grade:** | 1 | 2 | 3 | 4 | 5 | 6 | 7 | 8 | 9 | 10 |

Chapter 4. Sales Blueprints

4. **Presenting Your Product or Service:** You have a clear, proven process of presentation that demonstrates the benefits of buying to your prospect.
   a. You begin with the established need and move step by step from the general to the specifics of what you sell.
   b. At the end of the presentation, your prospect is clear about what you sell, how much it costs, how it will benefit him or her, and how to proceed.

   Grade: 1 2 3 4 5 6 7 8 9 10

5. **Answering Objections:** You have thought through and identified each reason a prospect might give for not buying at the end of your presentation.
   a. You have developed a clear and compelling way to address each objection you receive.
   b. Once you have answered a particular objection, the prospect is satisfied and it never comes up again.

   Grade: 1 2 3 4 5 6 7 8 9 10

6. **Closing the Sale:** You are skilled and comfortable when it is time to ask the customer to buy, to take action on your offer.
   a. You have thought through and prepared your closing words in advance.
   b. You recognize buying signals and are prepared to close the sale as soon as it is clear the customer is ready to buy.

   Grade: 1 2 3 4 5 6 7 8 9 10

7. **Getting Resales and Referrals:** You have a successful plan to get resales and referrals from each customer.
   a. You have several proven referral systems that bring you a "golden chain" of new prospects and customers.
   b. You have a "relationship management system" to keep in regular contact with your customers and good prospects.

   Grade: 1 2 3 4 5 6 7 8 9 10

8. **Personal Organizational Skills:** You are well organized, efficient, effective, and punctual every selling day.
   a. You plan and organize your months, weeks, and days in advance and set priorities on the use of your time.

WAY TO WEALTH WORKBOOK: BLUEPRINTS FOR BUSINESS SUCCESS

    b. You apply the 80/20 rule to everything you do and always concentrate on the highest-value use of your time.

Grade:	1	2	3	4	5	6	7	8	9	10

9. **Time and Territory Management:** You have a written plan to identify your best markets and prospects and you work your plan every day.
   a. You are clear about your target market, your ideal customers, who they are, where they are, why they buy, when they buy, and what benefits they seek.
   b. You plan your work and work your plan to ensure that you are spending the maximum amount of time possible with qualified prospects.

Grade:	1	2	3	4	5	6	7	8	9	10

10. **Personal and Professional Development:** You are continually working on your skills (the outer game) and your personality (the inner game) so you perform at your best.
    a. You continually read, listen to audio programs in your car, and attend selling seminars and courses.
    b. You make lifelong learning and growth a regular part of your personal and business life.

Grade:	1	2	3	4	5	6	7	8	9	10

Chapter 4. Sales Blueprints

Summary and Conclusions

Area	Score
1. Prospecting	
2. Building Rapport and Trust	
3. Identifying Needs	
4. Presenting Your Product or Service	
5. Answering Objections	
6. Closing the Sale	
7. Getting Resales and Referrals	
8. Personal Organizational Skills	
9. Time and Territory Management	
10. Personal and Professional Development	
Total Score	

Add up your scores from all 10 skill areas. Divide your total by 10 to get your rating.

    Score: 91–100 = Superstar

                  81–90 = Excellent

                  71–80 = Above Average

                  61–70 = Average Sales/Income

                  Below 60 = Below Average

You need an overall score of at least 70 to succeed in sales in today's competitive environment. You should be able to give yourself a score of 7 or above in each area.

Key point: Your weakest key skill area sets the height of your income. You could be "excellent" in several areas, but if you are weak in one of the above areas, that one area will largely determine your overall level of sales and income.

Question: What one skill, if you were excellent at it, would help you the most to increase your sales?

_____

_____

WAY TO WEALTH WORKBOOK: BLUEPRINTS FOR BUSINESS SUCCESS

2. Sales Planning Process

There is a basic rule in time management: Every minute spent in planning saves ten minutes in execution. The more time you invest to plan out your sales activities, the less time you waste, and the more prospects you see.

The basic rule for sales success is: "Spend more time with better prospects."

When you take the time to think through your sales work before you begin, you will become one of the most productive and highest paid salespeople in your field.

Idealization: Start your planning with a vision of your ideal result.

1. Describe your **perfect customer**.

    1. Age? _____

    2. Occupation? _____

    3. Income level? _____

    4. Education? _____

    5. Marital status? _____

    6. Attitude toward you? _____

    7. Location? _____

2. Define your **perfect customer experience**. What must happen for your customer to be happy?

    a. **Your product:** Features and benefits?

    1. _____

    2. _____

    3. _____

    b. **Your service:** People, treatment?

    1. _____

    2. _____

    3. _____

Chapter 4. Sales Blueprints

    c. **Your prices and terms?**

        1. _____

        2. _____

        3. _____

    d. **Your company:** What is your reputation?

        1. _____

        2. _____

        3. _____

3. What does your *perfect* customer consider **value**?

    1. _____

    2. _____

    3. _____

4. Why does your *perfect* customer buy from you? What **results or benefits** does he or she expect to enjoy?

    1. _____

    2. _____

    3. _____

5. What **qualities** do you have that attract ideal customers to you?

    1. _____

    2. _____

    3. _____

6. What **additional services** do you need to develop to attract more *ideal* customers?

    1. _____

    2. _____

    3. _____

Way to Wealth Workbook: Blueprints for Business Success

7. What can you do to *deserve* more and better **referrals** from your customers?

   1. _____

   2. _____

   3. _____

8. Based on your answers to the above, how would you **describe** your perfect prospect?

   1. _____

   2. _____

   3. _____

9. What must your ideal prospect be **convinced** of before he or she will buy from you?

   1. _____

   2. _____

   3. _____

10. What can you **do immediately** to attract and keep more and better customers?

    1. _____

    2. _____

    3. _____

What one action are you going to take immediately based on your answers to the above questions?

_____

_____

Chapter 4. Sales Blueprints

3. Seven Ways of Selling

1. **Simple Selling:** This is the traditional method, based on the **AIDA formula**:

   A. Attention: Your opening comment or headline must break the preoccupation of the prospect and get him or her to pay attention to you.

   I. Interest: You arouse interest by explaining the features of your products or services, what has gone into them to make them what they are.

   D. Desire: You arouse buying desire by explaining the benefits the customer will enjoy by buying and using your products or services.

   A. Action: You elicit action by asking the customer to make a decision and then close the sale.

   You can plan every sales presentation or advertisement with these four key ideas.

2. **Complex Selling:** This method is used to sell larger, more complex, and more expensive products or services. It has several stages:

   a. **Prospecting:** Finding qualified prospects who have a genuine need that your products or services can satisfy right now.

   b. **Establishing rapport and trust:** Taking the time to ask questions and learn about the prospect so that he or she feels confident in buying from you.

145

c. **Identifying needs accurately:** Asking questions and listening carefully to the answers so that you are clear about the prospect's true needs and situation.

___

___

d. **Presenting:** Showing the prospect that your product or service is ideal for him or her at this time.

___

___

e. **Answering objections:** Dealing effectively with the doubts and concerns that might cause the prospect to hesitate to buy.

___

___

f. **Closing the sale:** Asking for the buying decision with confidence and wrapping up the order.

___

___

g. **Getting resales and referrals from satisfied customers:** The true test of excellent sales skills and customer satisfaction.

___

___

How could you improve in each of these areas?

1. ___

2. ___

3. ___

Chapter 4. Sales Blueprints

3. **Relationship Selling:** This approach is based on building trust with the prospect. There are four stages:

    a. **Building trust** by asking questions and listening intently to the answers.

    b. **Identifying needs** by asking questions about the customer and his or her situabtion rather than talking about your product.

    c. **Presenting** by matching the customer's stated needs to your product features and benefits.

    d. **Confirming and closing** by asking the prospect to make a decision.

    Rule: Listening builds trust. In relationship selling, your job is to ask good questions and then listen attentively to answers.

Four Keys to Effective Listening

   1. **Listen attentively.** Do not interrupt while the prospect is speaking.
   2. **Pause before replying.** Take time to reflect on the prospect's words.
   3. **Question for clarification.** Ask, "How do you mean?"
   4. **Feed it back in your own words.** This proves that you were genuinely listening.

4. **Consultative Selling:** This is where you position yourself as a consultant, expert, and advisor on your product.

    a. Your job is to find a way to improve the customer's financial situation with your product or service.

    b. You sell "financial improvement" in that you seek ways either to increase sales, revenues, and profits or to reduce costs.

Way to Wealth Workbook: Blueprints for Business Success

    c. Your goal is to find a way to help your prospect with your product or service so that he or she receives more back in financial improvement than your product or service costs.

_____

_____

    You must answer your customer's **four key questions**:

        1. How much does it cost? _____

        2. How much do I get back? _____

        3. How fast do I get it back? _____

        4. How sure is this expected return? _____

    d. Your job in consultative selling is to demonstrate that your product or service pays for itself.

_____

_____

    e. Your main responsibility after the sale is to ensure that your customer receives the value or benefit that you promised.

_____

_____

5. **Value-based Selling:** Your job is to demonstrate why it is in the customer's best interests to pay more for your product than to buy a lower-priced product from a competitor.

    You must focus on the reasons for buying covered in the last section and incorporate them into your selling process.

6. **Educational Selling:** This is the process by which you teach the prospect what your product or service can do to give the prospect the benefits and results he desires.

    The basic method consists of three steps:

    a. **"Because of this":** You describe the product feature.
    b. **"You can":** You describe the product benefit.

Chapter 4. Sales Blueprints

c. **"Which means":** You describe the customer benefit, which is the reason that the customer would buy.

Example: You are selling a large computer monitor. "Because of this wide screen (product feature), you can *see your work more easily and with less eye strain* (product benefit), which means *you can do more and better work without stress or fatigue* (customer benefit).

7. **Solution-Selling or Customer-Centric Selling:** This is the process whereby you uncover a problem or need of the prospect, agree upon the ideal solution, show that your product or service offers that solution, and then give examples of how your product or service has brought about that result for other, similar customers.

Notes

WAY TO WEALTH WORKBOOK: BLUEPRINTS FOR BUSINESS SUCCESS

4. Seven Qualities of Top Salespeople

Give yourself a grade of 1–10 on each of these qualities. Your weakest key area determines the level of success in selling.

1. **Ambitious:** Top salespeople are "hungry." They are determined to succeed, to be the best at their profession. _____

2. **Optimistic:** Top salespeople have a positive mental attitude. They look for the good in every situation and strive to learn from every problem or difficulty. They expect the best continually. _____

3. **Courageous:** Top salespeople are willing to confront their fears of failure and rejection. They do the thing they fear over and over until their fear goes away. _____

4. **Committed:** Top salespeople believe in their products or services, in their companies, and in their customers. They put their whole heart into their work. _____

5. **Professional:** Top salespeople see themselves as consultants, advisors, helpers, and teachers. _____

6. **Dedicated:** Top salespeople are committed to continuous learning and self-improvement. They read constantly in the field of selling, listen to audio programs in their cars, and attend sales training seminars and courses regularly. _____

7. **Responsible:** Top salespeople see themselves as the presidents of their own professional sales corporations. They refuse to complain or make excuses. They say, "If it's to be, it's up to me!" _____

Notes
_____
_____
_____
_____
_____

Chapter 4. Sales Blueprints

5. Seven Best Sales-Closing Techniques

Your ability to ask for the order and close the sale determines your level of sales and your income. Fortunately, all closing skills are learned with practice and repetition. You must have the courage to "ask."

1. **Invitational Close:** "Why don't you give it a try?"

2. **Alternative Close:** "Which of these would you prefer?"

3. **Secondary Close:** You get agreement on a smaller part of your offering, a "yes" to which means that he has decided to buy: "Would you like this sent to your home or your office address?"

4. **Directive Close:** With this popular method, you assume the prospect has decided to buy: You ask, "Do you like this so far?" When the prospect says, "Yes" you close with these words: "Well then, the next step is (describe the plan of action) and I'll take care of all the details."

5. **Sharp Angle Close:** You use this technique to close on an objection. When the prospect objects to buying for whatever reason, you say, "If we could take care of (objection) for you, would you take it?"

6. **Authorization Close:** When you have spoken with the prospect several times and he or she still hasn't made a decision, you fill out your order form with all the details, exactly as you have discussed them. You then go back to the prospect and say, "Mr./Ms. Prospect, I've prepared this order exactly as we have discussed it. If you'll just authorize this, we can get started right away." You then push the order form across the desk, place your pen on top, and wait silently for him or her to make a decision, one way or another.

7. **Trial Close:** You use this technique throughout your presentation to get feedback and information. The best part of this close is that it can be answered with a "No" without ending the sale.

   "Do you like this color?"

   "No, not at all."

   "That's all right; we have several other colors." You continue with your presentation.

   The most important word in selling is "ask." Never be afraid to ask for a buying decision.

6. Four Levels of Customer Service

The purpose of selling is to create and keep a customer. Your ability to take excellent care of your customers is the key to your future. There are four levels of customer service you can strive for:

1. **You meet expectations.** This is the minimum level for you to stay in business. What are the most important expectations that your customers have of you and what you sell?

   1. _____
   2. _____
   3. _____

2. **You exceed expectations.** At this level, you do something for your customers that is unexpected and that makes them happy. What are three ways that you can exceed customer expectations?

   1. _____
   2. _____
   3. _____

3. **You delight your customers.** At this level, you are moving toward rapid business growth and greater profitability. In what ways do you, or could you, delight your customers?

   1. _____
   2. _____
   3. _____

4. **You amaze your customers.** At this level, you turn your customers into advocates out selling for you by telling everyone about your business. How do you, or could you, amaze your customers?

   1. _____
   2. _____
   3. _____

Chapter 4. Sales Blueprints

Here's the **ultimate question:** "Would you recommend us to others?"

"On a scale of 1–10, based on your experience with us, would you recommend us to your family and friends?"

Those customers who rate you and your business either 9 or 10 will represent 85% of your repeat business and referrals.

Question: What could you do with every customer to ensure a 9 or a 10 rating on this question?

1. _____
2. _____
3. _____

Notes

WAY TO WEALTH WORKBOOK: BLUEPRINTS FOR BUSINESS SUCCESS

7. Seven Keys to Effective Networking

Your sales success will often be determined by how many people you know and how many people know you in a favorable way. Top salespeople are continually broadening their network of contacts in every way possible.

To network effectively, use the following methods:

1. Join one or more **business organizations or associations** and attend meetings regularly. What three organizations could you join that contain potential customers?

    1. _____
    2. _____
    3. _____

2. Volunteer for service on one or more **key committees** of the organization. List three committees that contain the kind of people you would like to meet.

    1. _____
    2. _____
    3. _____

3. Introduce yourself to other members and ask them about their business and how they are doing. Resolve to meet **three new people** at each meeting.

    1. _____
    2. _____
    3. _____

4. Make no attempt to talk about **yourself** or your product. Instead, ask questions and talk to other people about their businesses.

5. Ask this **key question** of each new acquaintance: "Tell me what I would need to know about your product or service so I can recommend one of my friends or customers to you."

6. At the first opportunity, send the new acquaintance a prospect or customer.

7. Always look for ways to create business for others; they will always look for ways to reciprocate.

Chapter 4. Sales Blueprints

8. Seven Questions to Set Priorities in Selling

The greater clarity you have with regard to what you want and what you will have to do to achieve it, the faster you will achieve your sales and personal goals.

1. How much do you want to earn each month and each year?

    Per month? _____

    Per year? _____

2. How much will you have to sell each month and each year to earn this amount?

    Sell each month? _____

    Sell each year? _____

3. What is your average size of sale and amount of commission?

    Average size of sale? _____

    Average commission or income per sale? _____

4. How many *individual* sales will you have to make each week, each month, and each year to achieve your financial goals?

    Sales per week? Amount? _____

    Sales per month? Amount? _____

    Sales per year? Amount? _____

5. How many customers will you have to see, how many presentations/proposals will you have to make to achieve this level of sales?

    Customer contacts per week? _____

    Dollar amount of sales per month? _____

    Amount of sales per year? _____

6. How many calls will you have to make each day, each week, and each month to achieve that number of customer meetings and presentations?

    Calls per day? _____

    Calls per week? _____

    Calls per month? _____

7. What is your plan to make this number of calls, presentations, and sales each day, each week, or each month?

   1. _____
   2. _____
   3. _____
   4. _____
   5. _____

Keep track of your numbers in each of these areas. Make a note each time you make a call, a presentation, or a sale. Over time, these numbers will enable you to manage yourself and improve your performance.

Rule: What gets measured gets done. If you can't measure it, you can't manage it.

Notes

CHAPTER FIVE

Financial Blueprints

Every business activity can be expressed in financial terms. The more accurate you become with each of the financial measures of your business, the better decisions you will make and the better results you will get.

Continually imagine that you are going to appear before a bank board or a lending committee, and they are going to ask you to explain all the critical numbers in your business and how you obtained them.

Be your own banker or management consultant. Demand proof and back-up for every number in your business. Accept nothing on faith. Refuse to rely on luck or hope for the best. All successful businesspeople pay close attention to the numbers that explain the activities and operations of their businesses.

In this chapter:

1. Critical Success Factors, Benchmarks, and Metrics	159
2. 23 Ways to Get the Money You Need	161
3. Borrowing from Your Bank	169
4. Profit Analysis and Maximization	172
5. Double Your Income Seven Ways	174
6. Double Your Income—Exercises	176
7. Fifteen Profit-Making Strategies	178
8. Determining Your Costs	185

Way to Wealth Workbook: Blueprints for Business Success

9. Conduct a Breakeven Analysis	188
10. Twelve Ways to Set Your Prices	189
11. The Seven Systems You Need	196
12. Seven Keys to Legal Agreements	200
13. Rules Learned from Lawsuits and Arbitration	201

Chapter 5. Financial Blueprints

1. Critical Success Factors, Benchmarks, and Metrics

One of the most important parts of financial planning and setting up business systems is to determine measures, metrics, and scorecards for every job and for every part of every job.

These are often called "key success measures" or "critical success indicators." These are numbers that you can use for any activity to determine whether or not that activity has been carried out satisfactorily.

Your Economic Denominator

In every business, there is a critical number that is the key to the success or failure of the enterprise. This is your "economic denominator." The economic denominator in a business is the number that most accurately measures and determines the success of that business.

In some businesses, the economic denominator is the number of prospects who phone for further information as the result of advertising and promotion activities. In other businesses, it is the number of prospective customers who walk through the door of the store or shop seeking information on a product or service being offered. The economic denominator can be the number of sales that the company makes each day, the average size of the sales that are made daily, or the total sales volume.

The Measure of Success

What is your economic denominator? This is like the bull's-eye in the target that you are aiming at. What is the one number that more than anything else indicates the financial health of your business?

Personal Standards and Goals

Each person in your business should have an economic denominator. Each should have a key success indicator or metric that he or she can use to assess his or her performance. This number should be clear, visible, and objective. Everyone should know what it is and be able to determine whether that number is being reached regularly. This is the answer to the question, "How do I measure success at my job?"

Remember the Basics

In business, there are three basic activities:

1. Market and sell the product or service.

2. Produce and deliver the product or service that you have sold.
3. Manage and administer the money and activities of your business.

Whenever a company runs into trouble, it is because of a problem in one or more of these three critical areas.

The highest-paid work in business is thinking. Your ability to gather the information necessary to create a complete business plan, to think through the critical issues of your business, and to determine the critical success factors of your business will determine your success or failure more than any other factor.

Make a list of the most important numbers in your business, the ones you watch the most and that mean the most to the health of your business:

1. Number of prospects? _____

2. Number of responses to your advertising? _____

3. Number of sales? _____

4. Size of each sale? _____

5. Profit margin on each sale? _____

6. Frequency of purchase? _____

7. Number of referrals? _____

Of all these numbers, which is the most important? _____

Notes

Chapter 5. Financial Blueprints

2. 23 Ways to Get the Money You Need

Your business needs money at every stage of its existence, and your ability to get the money you need will largely determine your success or failure. There are many ways for you to raise money, from the beginning of your business until you retire.

1. **Dip into your savings.** First, and usually the most important, is your personal savings account. It is important for you to save money. If you cannot discipline yourself to save and accumulate money to get started, you probably do not have the character and discipline to succeed once your business gets going. What personal sources of money do you have for your business?

    1. _____
    2. _____
    3. _____

2. **Sell some assets.** Second, you can raise money by selling assets. You can sell your boat, your car, your motor home, or some of your furniture. You can sell everything or anything else that you own. You can cash in your life insurance. Sometimes you can sell stocks, bonds, or securities or liquidate your retirement account to get cash to start your business. What assets can you sell to invest in your business?

    1. _____
    2. _____
    3. _____

3. **Use your credit cards.** The third source of money that you can tap into to start or build your business is credit cards. Many of the most successful businesses in America were started by people who took out as many credit cards as possible while they were working, built up a solid credit rating, and then borrowed against and lived off those credit cards for two or three years until their businesses became profitable. What credit cards do you have or that you can get with high borrowing limits?

    1. _____
    2. _____
    3. _____

Way to Wealth Workbook: Blueprints for Business Success

4. **Take out personal loans.** The fourth source of money is personal loans. These are loans that are made to you on the basis of your job, your past credit rating, and your character. Sometimes you can get a personal line of credit from the bank, based on your assets. You can then use this line of credit to underwrite your business until you achieve sufficient sales and profitability. What are three personal loans that you could take out?

   1. _____
   2. _____
   3. _____

5. **Borrow against collateral.** Fifth, you can borrow money by taking out a collateral loan. You can borrow against something you own, such as a car, furniture, a boat, or a motor home. You can even borrow against your house. Many businesses have been started by the business owner mortgaging, financing, or borrowing against every single thing he or she owned. What property or collateral do you have that you could borrow against?

   1. _____
   2. _____
   3. _____

6. **Acquire love money.** The sixth basic source used to finance as many as 90% of new businesses is love money. This is money that people give you because they love you. This is money from friends, relatives, business associates, your parents, and other relatives. Who do you know who would or could lend money or invest in your business?

   1. _____
   2. _____
   3. _____

7. **Get a business loan.** The seventh source of money to get started is a business loan. Business loans require liquid asset coverage of at least $2 for every $1 that you wish to borrow. Business loans also require a minimum of one to two years of successful business history. To borrow money for your business, you will need

Chapter 5. Financial Blueprints

up-to-date financial statements, plus personal guarantees that cover everything that you own or ever will own. What could you do, starting today, to qualify for a business loan?

1. _____

2. _____

3. _____

8. **Bootstrap your way to success.** The eighth way to finance a business, one of the most popular and effective ways in business history, is bootstrapping. Bootstrapping requires that you start small, make sales and profits, reinvest your profits back into your business, and then make more sales and repeat the process.

    The advantage of bootstrapping is that you learn far faster than if you started with a lot of money. You replace financial capital with sweat equity. How could you bootstrap your way into your own business?

    1. _____

    2. _____

    3. _____

9. **Use customer financing.** The ninth way you can finance your business is with customer financing. Your customers pay in advance so you have the money to produce the goods and services that you sell to them.

    Ross Perot, who is today a multibillionaire, started Electronic Data Systems (EDS) with $1,000 borrowed from his mother ("love money"). After dozens of sales calls, he finally found one customer who would buy into his idea of handling all of the computer services of the customer corporation. Perot talked his first customer into paying 50% of the fees in advance so that Perot could afford to purchase the equipment and deliver the services in the first place. The rest is history. What terms of conditions could you offer a custoer to induce him to pay you in advance?

    1. _____

    2. _____

    3. _____

10. **Request a deposit.** Many companies will request a 50% deposit on an order when they make the sale. With this money, they will then buy the raw materials and pay for the labor to produce the product that they have sold. Their profit is contained in the other 50% that they collect on successful delivery of the product or service. How much of a deposit could you ask for each time you take an order?

   1. _____

   2. _____

   3. _____

11. **Get paid first.** Customer financing is a popular way of raising capital. For example, franchising is a form of customer financing. The franchisor expands the business by selling the right to use his business system and name in another market area. The franchisee pays a franchise fee that provides the money necessary to support the newly franchised business. McDonald's now has more than 30,000 franchises worldwide based on this concept of customer financing. How could you franchise your business or license your business concept to raise capital?

   1. _____

   2. _____

   3. _____

12. **Sell a subscription.** Another way of customer financing is the sale of newsletters, seminars, and subscriptions of any kind. The customers pay for the product or service in advance, prior to delivery. With a subscription, customers pay for the entire year of the product prior to receiving the first issue. How could you package your products or services so that customers pay for them in advance?

   1. _____

   2. _____

   3. _____

13. **Use direct mail marketing.** Direct mail marketing is another form of customer financing. Your up-front investment is in the advertising, but then you take the orders before you fill them and deliver the product. You receive the money by cash or credit card before you have to purchase and deliver the product or serv-

Chapter 5. Financial Blueprints

ice. Your customers are actually paying for the business as you go along. What could you sell by direct mail, getting paid first, and then fulfilling the order?

1. _____

2. _____

3. _____

14. **License the rights.** You can use customer financing by licensing the right to manufacture or market a product that you own or control in exchange for a royalty or a fee. What products or services or business methods do you have that other people will pay for the right to use or sell in their market areas?

1. _____

2. _____

3. _____

15. **Get a retainer.** Ask the customer to pay for your services in advance. You can use this type of customer financing in consulting. Many small businesses start with a person who has expert knowledge in a particular area. He or she goes out and offers his or her services as a consultant on what is called a "retainer basis." On this basis, the client pays you a monthly retainer to work with them for a certain number of days or hours each month. In exchange, they give you progress payments, usually on the first of the month. How could you sell your services on a retainer basis?

1. _____

2. _____

3. _____

16. **Consider multi-level marketing.** Multi-level marketing is another popular method of customer financing. In multi-level marketing all you require is a sample kit to get started. By demonstrating the samples, you can take orders and collect payment. You can then buy the products from the manufacturer, deliver the

orders, and keep the profits. What sort of multi-level products or companies do you know that you could represent to others?

1. _____

2. _____

3. _____

17. **Use customer financing.** Many companies use various forms of customer financing to get started. They make the sale and ask the customer to pay for all or part of the order when the order is placed. If this is not possible, they get the customer to agree to pay upon delivery of the order, rather than waiting 30, 60 or 90 days. They then take this money and pay their suppliers. How could you take advantage of customer financing?

    1. _____

    2. _____

    3. _____

18. **Factor your receivables.** Many companies will factor their purchase orders from their customers. Especially if you receive an order from a large company with a good reputation, the purchase order is virtually a guarantee to pay when you deliver the product or service that you have sold.

    Because of the creditworthiness of the customer, banks will lend you 70% or 80% of the face value of the order and then charge you an interest rate for carrying the balance between the time that they give you the money and the time you collect the money from your customer and repay the bank.

19. **Raise venture capital.** Venture capital is sophisticated money managed by experienced people that is pooled as risk capital to invest in potentially fast-growth companies. This type of money is famous but very hard to get.

    Many young entrepreneurs try to raise venture capital to start their businesses. They are amazed at how difficult this is. Fewer than 1% of business start-ups are financed by venture capital because they are so risky. Fully 99% of all business plans and proposals submitted to venture capitalists are eventually thrown in the wastebasket. Venture capitalists are not in the business of losing money for their clients.

    Venture capitalists will only invest in a business today when it has three things going for it: first, it has to have a proven success record. The business has to

Chapter 5. Financial Blueprints

have been in operation successfully for at least two years. At this stage, the business owner approaches venture capitalists for money to expand the business and to take advantage of larger market opportunities.

Second, the entrepreneur or business owner must submit a complete business plan. A complete business plan may take anywhere from two to six months to produce, and may require from 100 to 300 hours. It may cost anywhere from $25,000 to $50,000 to have it done by an outside consultant. The venture capitalist will not even talk to a person without a complete, detailed business plan that the entrepreneur thoroughly understands and can explain, page for page, number for number.

The third ingredient that venture capitalists look for before they will advance you any money is a competent management team in place. In fact, venture capitalists look more closely at the experience of the managers of the company than at any other factor when making a decision to lend money.

Therefore, if you do not have a proven success record of building and operating a profitable business, plus a complete business plan explaining exactly why you want the money and what you intend to do with it, plus a competent, proven management team in place, it is better to look for other sources of capital than from venture capitalists.

20. **Consult the Small Business Administration.** Another source of money that you can tap into is the Small Business Administration, or the SBA. The SBA will look at business plans as what is called a "lender of last resort." This means that they will only consider your business plan and your loan application when you have been turned down or rejected by at least two other banks or financial institutions.

21. **Seek funding from Small Business Investment Companies.** You can often raise money through small business investment companies (SBICs). These are risk groups that put together pools of money to invest in small, up and coming companies. They are similar to venture capital groups in that they require some kind of a track record before they will invest with you.

22. **Issue a public stock offering.** You can raise money for your business by a public stock offering. During the dotcom boom, many companies were going to market, selling stock, and raising large amounts of money even before they had built or sold a single product or service. As it happens, this type of investing, going public in advance of starting the business had never happened before, and will probably never happen again.

When your business is profitable, with a proven track record of sales and profits, and you need additional money to grow, you can go public by issuing shares and listing on a stock exchange. This is a sophisticated way of raising money and requires that you study it in detail. It is time-consuming and expensive, but it is one of the best ways to become rich as a business owner.

23. **Obtain supplier financing.** You can raise cash for your business by using what is called "supplier financing." Many companies that supply you with goods and services to sell to your customers will offer you delayed billing, if you ask for it. If you have a good track record and credit rating with your suppliers, they will often be willing to wait 60 or 90 days for payment. This gives you an opportunity to purchase products and services, even raw materials, from your suppliers, to produce the goods and services that you have sold to your customers, and then to get paid for them, all before payment is due to your suppliers.

Be Creative

Throughout your business career, you must continually think about where you will get the money or credit you need to survive and grow. The more of these methods you know and apply, the greater the likelihood that you will be successful in your business.

Notes

Chapter 5. Financial Blueprints

3. Borrowing from Your Bank

Throughout your business life, you will need to deal with banks for many reasons, especially for loans and lines of credit. Your ability to work effectively with your bank can make or break your business.

The Facts of Life

Business loans require liquid asset coverage of at least $2 for every $1 that you wish to borrow. Business loans also require a minimum of one to two years of successful business history. To borrow money for your business, you will need up-to-date financial statements and personal guarantees that cover everything that you own or ever will own.

Many people will tell you not to give personal guarantees when you take out a loan for your business. This is silly. Before a bank will lend you money for your business, the banker will not only want personal guarantees from you, but also from your spouse and often from your parents. Banks are not in the business of taking risks.

There are **five factors** that banks look for before they will make a loan to you or to any other businessperson:

1. They look for **collateral**. What assets are you going to put up to cover the loan? Collateral is something that the bank can sell for cash fairly quickly in case your business is not successful. What collateral do you have to pledge for a bank loan?

    1. _____

    2. _____

    3. _____

2. They look for **character.** How honest and dependable are you? Who knows you? Who will vouch for you?

    1. _____

    2. _____

    3. _____

Way to Wealth Workbook: Blueprints for Business Success

3. Banks look at your current **credit rating.** How good is your credit history? What amounts of money have you borrowed and repaid?

    1. _____
    2. _____
    3. _____

    Your credit rating follows you your entire life. Many people have ruined their entire adult lives because they have been sloppy or indifferent with their credit. They have failed to pay credit card bills or make car payments, utility payments, or rent payments. Their creditors have reported them to a national credit bureau. This negative credit rating has then dogged them for as long as 10 years, wherever they went, anywhere in the country. Don't let this happen to you.

4. Banks look for your **capital.** How much of your own money are you willing to invest? This is a measure of how deeply committed you are to the enterprise. What capital assets do you have to invest or borrow against?

    1. _____
    2. _____
    3. _____

5. The fifth factor that banks look for is **confidence** in you. In the final analysis, a banker must be confident that you are going to succeed in the business that he or she is lending you money to start or build. What are the three best reasons for a banker to have confidence in you?

    1. _____
    2. _____
    3. _____

Build Your Banking Relationships Slowly

Borrowing money from banks is a progressive series of financial transactions that develop over time. When you first attempt to borrow money, most banks will want $5 of assets, collateral, personal investments, and other assets for every $1 that they will lend you. They will also want personal guarantees that extend beyond bankruptcy, should you declare it. But after a bank has several

Chapter 5. Financial Blueprints

years of experience with you and comes to know you and trust you, its lending requirements will decline, step by step.

After five years of lending you money and getting their money back with interest, a bank will lower its requirements for cash, collateral, assets, and even personal guarantees. The banker will be content for you to pledge the cash flow and the assets of your business to support the loans that you are taking out. At a certain point, the bank will even come to you and offer to lend you more money to expand your business or to make other investments.

Notes

4. Profit Analysis and Maximization

To maximize the profits from your business, you must continually study and analyze your income, costs, the profitability of each part of your enterprise.

1. 80% of your profits will come from 20% of your products, services, and customers. What are your three most profitable products or services?

    1. _____

    2. _____

    3. _____

2. How much of your three most profitable products or services do you sell each month? How much each year?

    1. Each month? _____ Each year? _____

    2. Each month? _____ Each year? _____

    3. Each month? _____ Each year? _____

3. Add up every cost of making those sales.
   _____
   _____

4. Determine the net profit you earn from the sales of each product or service.
   _____
   _____

5. Organize your products and services in order to the most profitable to the least profitable.
   _____
   _____

6. Identify the low-profit, no-profit products and services and decide to raise their prices, lower their costs, or discontinue them.
   _____
   _____

Chapter 5. Financial Blueprints

7. Focus all your marketing and sales activities on selling more of your most profitable products and services.

Notes

5. Double Your Income Seven Ways

There are seven ways to double your income in your business. You can apply one more of these methods every day and every week.

1. **Make more sales.** You can increase the number of sales you make each day, month, and year. How could you increase the total volume of your sales?

    1. _____
    2. _____
    3. _____

2. **Make larger sales.** You can increase the size of each sale via up-selling, cross-selling, discounting, and bonuses. How could you make larger sales to each customer?

    1. _____
    2. _____
    3. _____

3. **Make more profitable sales.** You can sell more profitable products or services or sell your current products at a higher profit. How could you earn higher profits on your sales?

    1. _____
    2. _____
    3. _____

4. **Sell more often to the same customers.** You can increase the frequency with which your customers buy from you. How could you get your customers to buy more often?

    1. _____
    2. _____
    3. _____

Chapter 5. Financial Blueprints

5. **Raise your prices.** You can raise the prices of both your top-selling products and your slower-selling products. Which of your products could you charge more for?

   1. _____

   2. _____

   3. _____

6. **Reduce your costs.** You can examine every part of your business to find ways to squeeze out costs without reducing quality. In what ways could you decrease your costs of operations, or of the products or services you sell?

   1. _____

   2. _____

   3. _____

7. **Sell something else.** You can introduce new and completely different products to your current and future customers. What additional or different products or services could you sell?

   1. _____

   2. _____

   3. _____

You should continually review every aspect of your business activities to find ways to increase your sales and reduce your costs.

Notes

_____

_____

_____

_____

_____

Way to Wealth Workbook: Blueprints for Business Success

6. Double Your Income—Exercises

Answer the following questions along or with other members of your team. Decide on specific actions you are going to take.

1. List three ways you could increase the **number** of your sales right now.

    1. _____
    2. _____
    3. _____

2. List three ways you could increase the **size** of each sale.

    1. _____
    2. _____
    3. _____

3. List three ways you could increase the **profitability** of each sale.

    1. _____
    2. _____
    3. _____

4. List three ways you could get your customers to purchase from you **more frequently**.

    1. _____
    2. _____
    3. _____

5. List three ways that you could **raise your prices**.

    1. _____
    2. _____
    3. _____

Chapter 5. Financial Blueprints

6. List three ways you could **reduce your costs** immediately.

    1. _____

    2. _____

    3. _____

7. List three additional or **alternate products or services** you could offer.

    1. _____

    2. _____

    3. _____

What **one action** will you take immediately to double your sales and profitability based on your answers to these questions?

_____

_____

Notes

7. Fifteen Profit-Making Strategies

Your ability to generate sales and profits is the key to your success. Most businesses use only one or two profit-making strategies. Here are the most important ever discovered. Think about how you can apply them in your business.

1. **Lead generation:** This is the process that you use to attract interested prospects to your business. If five out of ten prospects who come into your place of business end up buying from you, and if you can increase the number of people coming in from ten to 15, you can increase your sales and profits by 50%.

   You must think about lead generation morning, noon, and night. The law of probabilities says that, if you increase your number of leads, you increase your probabilities of making more and better sales. In what three ways could you increase the number of leads you get?

   1. _____

   2. _____

   3. _____

2. **Lead conversion:** The process of turning leads into customers is the measure of the effectiveness of your sales efforts. If you can increase your conversion rate from one out of ten to two out of ten, you can double your sales and your profits.

   We have seen over and over that small changes in a single one of the seven Ps of the marketing mix can lead to dramatic changes in lead conversion, from one out of ten to eight out of ten, within 30 days. This improvement in a critical variable can be the difference for your business between struggling and becoming wealthy.

   Improving your ability to sell and convert interested prospects into paying customers is one of the most important things you do. There is no replacement for ongoing sales training, both for you and for every person who speaks with customers, either live or on the phone.

   Look at every part of your sales process and seek ways to improve a little bit in each area. Because of the compounding principle, a small improvement in each key area can lead to an enormous improvement in overall sales results. List three ways that you could convert more leads to sales in your business:

   1. _____

   2. _____

   3. _____

Chapter 5. Financial Blueprints

3. **Number of transactions:** By increasing the frequency of individual sales you make by 10%, you increase your sales and profitability by the same amount. What are some of the things that you could do to get your customers to buy from you more frequently?

    1. _____
    2. _____
    3. _____

4. **Size of transaction:** You should be continually looking for ways to sell more to each customer with each transaction. How could you increase the size of each purchase?

    1. _____
    2. _____
    3. _____

5. **Profit margin per sale:** This is your gross profit from the sale of each product or service. By continually seeking ways to increase the price or decrease the cost of the product or service without decreasing the quality, you can inch up your profits per sale.

    Remember: Every dollar increased in profits, holding everything constant, flows straight to your bottom line as net profit. Every dollar decreased in expenses, holding sales and revenues constant, also goes straight to your bottom line as net profit. What are three ways that you could increase your profit margin per sale?

    1. _____
    2. _____
    3. _____

6. **Cost of customer acquisition:** This is the average amount you have to pay to acquire each paying customer. You should be continually seeking creative ways to improve your advertising and promotion so that it costs you less to buy each

customer. This can have a dramatic impact on your profitability. How could you lower your average cost of customer acquisition?

1. _____

2. _____

3. _____

7. **Customer referrals:** These are the customers that come to you as the result of recommendations from satisfied customers. Your ability to develop one or more proven referral systems for your business can have a large impact on your sales and profitability.

It is 15 times easier to make a sale to a referral from a satisfied customer than it is to advertise, promote, cold call, and prospect to find customers. This means that it takes 1/15th of the time, energy, and expense to sell to a referral. Referral business is the best business that you can develop. How can you get more referrals from your current customers?

1. _____

2. _____

3. _____

Keep Asking the Ultimate Question

Remember the ultimate question: "On a scale of one to ten, would you recommend us to others?"

Ask your customers this question on a regular basis. If they give you a score below 9 or 10, ask them what you have to do to score 9 or 10 in their estimation. Then, whatever they tell you it would take for them to recommend you to others, find a way to do it.

Very often, customers who give you a low score will raise their score immediately if you just ask them for advice on improving your services to them. When you make the change that they suggest, the change that they said would cause them to send you referral business, report back to them and tell them what you have done. Thank them for their advice and input. This will tremendously increase their loyalty and lead to them becoming repeat customers.

Chapter 5. Financial Blueprints

How can you improve the quality of your customer service so you can get more referrals?

1. _____

2. _____

3. _____

8. **Eliminate costly services and activities:** Many companies get into a routine or rhythm of offering expensive services to their customers that could be easily discontinued with no loss of customer loyalty or satisfaction.

   Look at the little services that you offer to your customers. Is there anything that you could cut back or discontinue altogether? In our office, we used to have a full-time receptionist at a total cost of more than $2,000 per month. We installed a customer-friendly answering system that channels callers straight to a person with one touch of the button and we stopped using the receptionist. We have never received a question or complaint about our answering system and we save a substantial amount of money each month. Could you do something like this? List three costly services or costs that you could eliminate.

   1. _____

   2. _____

   3. _____

9. **Outsource business activities:** You should outsource every activity in your business that your customer does not want or need or is willing to pay for. This includes payroll, printing, janitorial services, computer services, maintenance, and other activities.

   Imagine taking your customers around your company and showing them everything you do. Imagine asking them, "Would you pay money for this function?" Whatever activities your customers would not pay for are candidates for outsourcing, downsizing, or eliminating.

   The fact is that outside companies that specialize in a particular service—one that is not your direct line of business—can usually perform it better and at a lower cost than you, when you add up all expenses. Keep thinking about streamlining your business down to your core functions and discontinuing or outsourcing everything else. What three functions or activities in your business could you outsource to another company?

1. _____

2. _____

3. _____

10. **Reduce people costs:** It is estimated that each person who works for you actually costs you at least three times his or her salary. An employee who is paid $25,000 a year actually costs about $75,000 per year, once you have included all of the benefits, sick pay, offices, utilities, gasoline, and other resources that he or she uses, plus the cost of the time it takes for you to supervise and manage that employee.

    In some companies and businesses, it costs as much as six times a person's annual salary to have him or her on the payroll. This is why companies that reduce turnover, which is very expensive, and reduce head count increase their profits immediately. In what three ways could you reduce your people costs?`

    1. _____

    2. _____

    3. _____

11. **Reduce fixed costs:** These are costs you incur each month even if you do not sell a single product or service. These include rent, wages of full-time staff, utilities, telephone charges, pre-paid advertising, and every other regular expense you incur.

    You must be continually seeking ways to reduce this number. Your fixed costs constitute the minimum profit that you have to reach each month to break even. List three ways that you could reduce your fixed costs.

    1. _____

    2. _____

    3. _____

Chapter 5. Financial Blueprints

12. **Increase variable costs:** A variable cost is a cost that you incur only when you make a sale. This can include the costs of the product, shipping and delivery, overnight postage, salespeople and sales commissions, and other forms of labor.

    In what ways could you increase variable costs and reduce fixed costs?

    1. _____

    2. _____

    3. _____

13. **Lower your breakeven point:** This is the number of items you must sell each month to break even or to make a profit. You determine your breakeven point by calculating your gross profit per item that you sell and then dividing that number into your monthly fixed costs.

    For example, if your monthly fixed costs are $10,000, whether you sell anything or not, and you earn $10 gross profit per item sold, after deducting the cost of goods sold and all selling costs, you divide $10 into $10,000 to get 1,000 units as your breakeven point for the month. This is the minimum quantity that you must sell to avoid losing money.

    You use this breakeven point to evaluate the potential effectiveness of any advertising or other expense that you incur to increase sales. Every expense to increase sales must be seen as an investment with an expected rate of return that is greater than the cost. What could you do to lower your breakeven costs?

    1. _____

    2. _____

    3. _____

14. **Raise your prices:** In many situations, you can raise your prices by 5% or 10% without experiencing any market resistance. If your products and services are of good quality and your employees are friendly and helpful, a small increase in your overall prices will not drive your customers away.

    Are your competitors charging higher prices for similar products and services? Which of your products and services are popular with your customers? What are three areas where you could raise your prices?

    1. _____

    2. _____

    3. _____

15. **Do a constraint analysis:** The principle of constraints is one of the most helpful you will ever learn to increase profits. This principle says that between you and any business goal there is a constraint—a choke point or a bottleneck—that determines the speed at which you achieve that goal.

1. _____

2. _____

3. _____

What sets the speed at which you double your profitability in your company? What is holding you back? Once you have identified the one thing that constrains your profits the most, you must focus single-mindedly on removing that limitation or solving that problem. One breakthrough, the alleviation of one critical constraint, can double your sales and your profits. What are your main constraints on increased sales and profitability?

Notes

Chapter 5. Financial Blueprints

8. Determining Your Costs

Many businesses go broke because of confusion on the part of the owner about costs. You have heard people jokingly say, "We lose money on every one, but we make it up on the volume." Unfortunately, there are many businesses that actually lose money on high sales volume because their costs are out of control. There are several costs you must consider:

1. **Direct costs:** The costs of goods sold. If you make a product or buy it from a manufacturer or distributor for $5, including all costs of shipping, transportation, insurance, and delivery, and you sell the product for $10, your cost of goods sold is $5. This is fairly easy to calculate.

   List three of your most important direct costs:

   1. _____

   2. _____

   3. _____

2. **Indirect costs:** The costs attributable to each product or service that you sell. Indirect costs can be costs of salaries, rent, telephones, utilities, marketing, advertising, shipping, delivery, and many others.

   Include every expense. On inspection, it may turn out that the costs of executive time, staff salaries, advertising, sales costs and commissions, shipping and delivery, insurance, and then returns because of product defects or customer dissatisfaction actually total up to a loss on every sale. This is why it is so important that you continually calculate and recalculate every dollar you spend per product or service that you sell.

   You need to consider the costs of returns, both shipping and delivery. You need to calculate "shrinkage," the value of your products or services that "disappear" in the course of business activities. You need to calculate breakage and defects. You need to calculate losses that come from writing off accounts from people who cannot or will not pay you for what you have sold them.

   In totaling your indirect costs, you need to determine how much you must allocate for follow-up services, maintenance, and repairs for the product or service you sell.

   In addition, you must calculate the outside services you require to operate your business, especially legal and accounting. You must calculate not only the labor costs and salaries of each staff member who must spend any amount of time producing, selling, or delivering the product or service, but you must also include your own labor at your hourly rate.

The average entrepreneur works about 2,000 hours per year. If your income target is $50,000 per year, divided by 2,000, this means that your desired hourly rate is $25. If your income goal is $100,000 per year, your hourly rate is $50. In determining your indirect costs, you must include the number of hours of your own time that go into making the sale. Otherwise, your true costs will be distorted and inaccurate.

List three of your most important indirect costs:

1. _____

2. _____

3. _____

3. **Fixed costs:** The costs you incur each month whether or not you sell a single item or generate a single dollar of revenue. Your fixed costs include salaries for your permanent staff, rent, utilities, many operational costs, and the costs for outside services, plus your own income from the business.

   You should calculate your fixed costs on a regular basis to determine how much it costs you to stay in business if you have no revenues at all. One of your business goals should be to continually find ways to reduce your fixed costs.

   What are your three largest fixed costs?

   1. _____

   2. _____

   3. _____

4. **Variable costs:** The costs that increase or decrease depending on your level of business activity. These costs are incurred only when a sale takes place. They can include costs of goods sold, sales commissions, delivery costs, and other costs that can be attributed, directly or indirectly, to the cost of each product or service you sell.

   What are your largest variable costs?

   1. _____

   2. _____

   3. _____

Chapter 5. Financial Blueprints

5. **Semi-variable costs:** The costs that are partially fixed and partially variable. They can include part-time labor when you are busier than normal, additional utility, telephone, and mailing costs, and additional costs for outside services.

   List three semi-variable costs:

   1. _____

   2. _____

   3. _____

6. **Sunk costs:** The expenses that you have incurred that are gone forever: they can never be recovered.

   Face the facts. Building a business is often a sloppy affair. No matter how smart you are, you will buy products that you cannot resell at any price. You will buy furniture that will turn out to be of no value to you. You will run advertisements and engage in other activities that will turn out to be a waste of money. In building a business, these mistakes are inevitable and unavoidable.

   It is essential that you recognize them for what they are—"sunk costs." The money is gone forever. You cannot recoup it. You must not spend a single dollar attempting to compensate for a financial mistake in the past. Focus on the future and on sales and profits.

   List three examples of sunk costs in your business:

   1. _____

   2. _____

   3. _____

Once you have accurately calculated all of these expenses—direct and indirect, fixed and variable, and semi-variable—you will have a precise cost for bringing each product or service to the market satisfactorily. With this number, you can then begin thinking about your pricing structure.

9. Conduct a Breakeven Analysis

It is essential that you know how much it costs you to stay in business each month and each year. The more closely you study your numbers, the better decisions you make regarding expenditures.

1. Determine how much it costs to run your business each month, whether or not you have a single dollar of sales.

   These are your fixed costs: _____

2. Determine how much net profit you earn from each sale: _____

3. Divide your net profit amount into your fixed monthly costs to get your breakeven point: _____

   Example: A. Monthly fixed costs: $10,000
   　　　　　　　B. Profit per sale: $100
   　　　　　　　C. Divide B into A =   100

   You must sell 100 units per month to break even.

4. **Goal:** lower your breakeven point.

   Methods: 1. Lower your monthly operating costs.
   　　　　　　　2. Increase your profit per sale.

5. Be clear about your breakeven costs every month.

Continually seek ways to reduce your break even point. Carefully consider every expense you incur that increases your fixed costs.

Notes

_____
_____
_____
_____
_____
_____

Chapter 5. Financial Blueprints

10. Twelve Ways to Set Your Prices

Your ability to charge the ideal, profit-maximizing price for each of your products or services is the key to business success.

Sometimes I ask business owners these questions:

- Who sets your prices?
- Who determines your profit margins?
- Who determines what you offer, to whom you offer it, and how much you sell?
- Who determines the entire course of your business in a competitive market?"

Almost invariably, the first response I get is "I do!"

Then, I gently point out, "Your *competition* determines how much you charge, how much you sell, to whom you sell it to, your profit margins, how fast you grow, and almost everything else about your business."

The Market Clearing Price

In economics, there is a concept called the "market-clearing price." This is the price at which demand and supply are balanced: all buyers can purchase all the products or services of a particular kind they want and all sellers can sell everything they offer. At the end of the day, everyone is satisfied. The market-clearing price is the ideal price in any market.

Pricing Models

There are various ways you can set your prices for your products or services. But you must always remember that these are "guesstimates" based on your knowledge of what your competition is charging and what your customers are likely to pay, combined with your intuition, your gut feeling, about what the market will bear.

The "entrepreneurial instinct" that makes you successful is your ability to perceive a gap between what customers will pay for your product or service and the total cost of bringing that product or service to the market. It is this "profit opportunity" that entrepreneurs can see and that most other people cannot see that is the spark that triggers entrepreneurial activity. The better you become at identifying this gap between sales price and cost, the more successful you become as an entrepreneur.

1. **Cost-Plus Markup:** In this model of pricing, you take your total cost and mark it up by a specific amount. Usually this is done on a percentage basis.

    Depending on competitive pressures and sales volume, companies will mark up

189

their products with different percentages. In jewelry, for example, because jewelry stores have to carry such large inventories, the markups can be several hundred percent. In groceries, because products turn over so fast, the markups are about 20% of wholesale costs. This is a convenient way to set your prices, especially at the beginning. But always keep your competitors' prices in mind.

With which products do you use cost-plus markup to set your prices?

1. _____

2. _____

3. _____

2. **Cost Plus:** When I built my first shopping center, the owner of the construction company explained to me their pricing practice. They said, "We take the total of construction and then add 10% for administration and 10% for profit."

    This is "cost-plus pricing." Many companies that offer services will total the entire cost, direct and indirect, of providing the service and then mark it up by a fixed percentage. Many contracts, large and small, are priced on a cost-plus basis. This might be appropriate for your business as well.

    Which of your products are suitable for cost-plus pricing?

    1. _____

    2. _____

    3. _____

3. **Multiple of Total Costs:** You calculate your total costs of production or costs of goods sold and multiply that by a specific number. If you manufacture a high-margin product or service, you could mark it up by five or even ten times the manufacturing cost. This is quite common.

    Many entrepreneurs do not realize that, because of all of the indirect and unexpected costs in their businesses, they can go broke marking up a product by 100%. They can buy a product for $10 and sell it for $20. But once they have deducted all the costs that go into getting that product to the customer, they find that they are losing money on every sale. Don't let this happen to you.

    Which of your products can you or do you price at a multiple of cost?

    1. _____

    2. _____

    3. _____

Chapter 5. Financial Blueprints

4. **Market Pricing:** This is perhaps the most common way of setting a price on a commonly used consumer product. Unless your product or service offers a valuable benefit not offered by your competitors, you will have to keep your prices within 10% of what your competitors are charging for the same product or service in the same market area.

   What are the competitive market prices for what you sell?

   1. _____

   2. _____

   3. _____

5. **Monopoly Prices:** These are prices that you can charge because no one else offers the same product or service as you do in that market area. As a result, you can charge premium prices, prices that are highly profitable to you, and customers who want your product or service have no choice but to pay you what you charge.

   The ability to charge monopoly or above-market prices comes about only because of the uniqueness and irreplaceable nature of your product or service. For example, you can often charge monopoly prices simply because your business is the only source of that product or service in your geographical location.

   Create your own "monopoly." One of the ways that you can charge monopoly prices is by creating a "monopoly" by designing or structuring your products or services in such a way that they are far more attractive and desirable than those of your competitors. That difference makes you the only choice for potential customers. The customer cannot think of going anywhere else.

   Become the preeminent choice. One of the questions that you must continually ask is "How can I structure my business or my offerings in such a way that I am the 'preeminent' choice for customers in my market?"

   What can you do to make your products or services so attractive so that your prospective customers see you as the best choice of all, the only choice, all things considered? By asking and answering this question continually, you may come up with a special way of doing business that gives you a competitive advantage. This advantage will enable you to charge premium prices and earn premium profits.

Way to Wealth Workbook: Blueprints for Business Success

List three ways you could structure your product or service offerings so that you are the only choice in your market:

1. _____

2. _____

3. _____

6. **Variable Prices:** Many companies charge different prices, at different times, for different reasons, for the same product or service. Their prices vary depending upon circumstances.

   For example, if you sell a single product or service to a single customer, your costs can be quite high in servicing that customer. In this case, you would charge full retail.

   On the other hand, if your customer were to buy a large volume of your products or services, your cost of servicing that customer would decline dramatically. In this case, you could offer substantial discounts for volume purchases, as many companies do. You could offer variable prices if people purchase from you more frequently.

   Prices vary according to time of purchase. Many companies charge variable prices based on the time of day, week, or even season or year that customers buy, such as movie theaters.

   Keeping the doors open. Often, companies will have spare capacity. They will have fixed costs of equipment, staff, rent, utilities, and other costs that must be paid. To defray these costs, they will often offer their products or services at deeply discounted prices, just above their total costs, to keep the staff working and the factories operating.

   The add-on or up sell. Another type of variable price sale is the add-on or up-sell. In this case, you can offer your product or service at a special price, as long as the customer buys something else, on which you also make a profit, at the same time.

   What are three ways you can offer variable pricing to increase your sales or to generate sales that you would otherwise miss?

   1. _____

   2. _____

   3. _____

Chapter 5. Financial Blueprints

7. **Walk-Away Price:** This is the price below which you will not sell your product or service. You should be clear about this number before you begin negotiating. This becomes the basis for your variable pricing. Below this amount, you incur losses that make it of no value for you to offer the product or service at all.

   Which are your three most popular products or services and what is the lowest price you would accept for each of them?

   1. _____
   2. _____
   3. _____

8. **Introductory or Loss-Leader Prices:** With this type of pricing, you consider the lifetime value of a customer. If, based on your experience, a customer who buys from you will buy from you several times over the coming months or years, you can often charge a loss-leader price to acquire the customer. This discount is simply a cost of doing business, a cost of "buying" a customer.

   In many cases, especially in retail or service businesses, it is common to lose money on the first sale. Because of the high costs of marketing, advertising, and selling commissions or expenses, plus your cost of goods sold, you can end up with a net loss on a sale once you have deducted all your costs. You often have no choice but to do this.

   However, if you are confident that this customer, if satisfied, will buy from you over and over, you can calculate the lifetime value of the customer and justify taking a loss in the first sale.

   What are three situations when you could break even or lose money to get a customer for the first time?

   1. _____
   2. _____
   3. _____

9. **Market Demand Pricing:** This is charging whatever you feel that the market will pay. If you have a competitive advantage of some kind, you can charge a premium because customers will willingly pay more to get the special features or benefits that you offer.

   Raising your prices. When should you raise your prices? The best time to raise your prices is when the market demand for what you are selling is almost greater than your capacity to deliver your products or services. If you are a serv-

193

ice company and you are fully booked, all day long, you can probably raise your prices without decreasing the demand.

If people are buying your products with both hands and you cannot keep enough of them in stock, this is a good sign that your products are underpriced based on what customers are willing to pay. In this case, you can gradually raise your prices, selectively or across the board. You continue raising your prices for your products or services until the demand slows down and balances out with the quantity of products and services you are prepared to supply.

What are three popular products or services for which you could raise your prices without decreasing your sales?

1. _____

2. _____

3. _____

10. **Breakeven Price:** This is the price at which you neither earn a profit nor take a loss. You sell the product for exactly what it cost you to produce it. You sell at the breakeven price only when you cannot charge any more and you do not have to charge any less.

    What are your breakeven prices for your three most popular products or services?

    1. _____

    2. _____

    3. _____

11. **Clearance Sale Price:** This is the price at which you admit that the market demand for the product or service you have produced is considerably less than you had anticipated. You have too many of your products in stock. They are taking up too much room and selling too slowly.

    At the clearance sale price, you bite the bullet and realize that "half a loaf is better than no loaf at all." You clear out your stock so that you can turn that "dead stock" into cash that you can then use to offer other products and services that are in greater demand and on which you can earn a greater profit.

Chapter 5. Financial Blueprints

Which three products should you sell off at any price so that you can sell more profitable products?

1. _____

2. _____

3. _____

12. **Pricing Flexibility:** This is an attitude rather than a method. Always remember that prices are subjective. They are guesses at what the market will bear. They are based on a variety of pieces of information that are continually changing.

    Your job is to sell as many of your products and services as possible, at the highest possible price, to yield the highest possible profits. But from the beginning to the end of your entrepreneurial career, you must be flexible with your prices and be prepared and willing to raise or lower them depending on market conditions.

    Sometimes, you can increase your prices a lot or a little and dramatically change the profitability of your business. In other cases, you can lower the price of your products or services and so increase your sales volume at a lower profit point such that your overall profits increase substantially.

    The key is to be flexible. Nothing is written in stone. Be open to new information. Be continually watching your competitors. Listen closely to your customers. Keep your finger on the pulse of the sales and profitability of your business.

    List three areas where it would help you to be more flexible in the amount you charge:

    1. _____

    2. _____

    3. _____

Continually examine and reexamine your prices from every angle to find way to sell more and generate higher profits. never be satisfied or content.

11. The Seven Systems You Need

To achieve maximum business success, you must put systems in place for every key activity. These systems are like recipes that everyone follows, every single time, in the performance of specific business activities.

Without systems, everyone performs every function differently, based on their level of training and personality. With written systems, it is easier for you to hire good people, train them quickly, and monitor their work to assure that everything is being done with maximum efficiency.

Here are the seven essential systems that you must have in your business:

1. **Lead Generation:** You need a proven system of marketing, advertising, and promotion that generates a steady steam of qualified leads, phoning your place of business, responding on the Internet, or personally coming into your store to buy your product or service. List seven steps that you follow to generate qualified sales leads for your business:

    1. _____
    2. _____
    3. _____
    4. _____
    5. _____
    6. _____
    7. _____

2. **Lead Conversion:** You need a proven sales system to convert interested prospects into buying customers. List the seven steps you follow to convert leads into sales:

    1. _____
    2. _____
    3. _____
    4. _____
    5. _____

Chapter 5. Financial Blueprints

    6. _____

    7. _____

3. **Production of the Product or Service:** You need a proven system, from beginning to end, to produce the product or service you have sold to the customer. What are the steps you follow to produce the product or service you sell?

    1. _____
    2. _____
    3. _____
    4. _____
    5. _____
    6. _____
    7. _____

4. **Delivery System:** You need a step-by-step system to fulfill orders and deliver the product or service to the customer in a timely fashion. What are the steps you follow to deliver your product or service?

    1. _____
    2. _____
    3. _____
    4. _____
    5. _____
    6. _____
    7. _____

5. **Service Systems:** You need written policies and procedures for follow-up service to each of your customers, including established ways to handle customer needs and complaints, to generate additional sales, to keep in regular customer contact, to elicit referrals and recommendations from satisfied customers to new

customers, and to alert your customers to new products and services that they may be interested in buying. What are the steps in your customer service system?

1. _____

2. _____

3. _____

4. _____

5. _____

6. _____

7. _____

6. **Accounting Systems:** You need smoothly functioning accounting systems that track every penny of revenue and expense coming into or moving out of the business. How do you track and account for money coming in and out of your business, purchasing supplies, and paying bills?

1. _____

2. _____

3. _____

4. _____

5. _____

6. _____

7. _____

7. **Hiring, Training, and Personnel Systems:** You need written systems that clearly describe each job and how it is to be done. List the steps in your hiring and training system for new employees.

1. _____

2. _____

3. _____

4. _____

Chapter 5. Financial Blueprints

5. _____

6. _____

7. _____

Failure to develop these essential systems can lead to mistakes, confusion, lost time and money, and even failure of the business. Each system should be written out, like an instruction manual that each new person can learn and follow. As you get more information and experience, you should upgrade these systems so that they remain current and applicable to your present situation.

Notes

12. Seven Keys to Legal Agreements

Every part of your business will be based on a legal agreement of some kind. Your ability to enter into these legal agreements in an intelligent way is essential to your success. The rule is that "understandings prevent misunderstandings." You must pay close attention to every detail in legal agreements and always assume that the worst can happen in the business arrangement.

Here are the key steps to follow:

1. Discuss every element of the agreement and reach understanding before committing the details to paper.
2. Put every detail of the agreement in writing, including how and where any disputes are to be resolved.
3. Write the terms and conditions of the agreement as if the two parties were to become bitter enemies in the future.
4. Write the agreement with specific performance measures that must be met by both parties to keep the agreement in force.
5. Have the agreement either prepared by a good lawyer or carefully reviewed by a lawyer before finalizing and signing.
6. Resolve clearly any vague or disputed terms or conditions of the agreement in writing before finalizing or signing.
7. Strictly enforce the terms of the agreement and strictly adhere to the terms. Document deviations in writing, duly signed by both parties.

Hire a good lawyer and have him review or even prepare every legal agreement. Experienced lawyers are usually familiar with every potential problem that can arise in a business contract, and can give you advice that will save you a good deal of money.

Notes

_____
_____
_____
_____
_____

Chapter 5. Financial Blueprints

13. Rules Learned from Lawsuits and Arbitration

We live in a litigious society where people think automatically of suing whenever they feel wronged or there is a misunderstanding. If you are in business of any kind, you are going to be sued by someone, for some reason.

Most lawsuits are frivolous and invalid. They are brought by plaintiff attorneys who work on contingency fees or commissions. Many lawsuits are attempts to extort money from the business owner who will pay to settle as an alternative to paying the costs to defend against the claim.

If ever you are sued, you must immediately get advice from a lawyer. If you act by yourself, you will probably become too emotional to make the best decisions.

Here are some rules that come from people who have been sued:

1. Never get into business with someone who needs you more than you need them.
2. Never hire anyone without absolute clarity concerning responsibilities and reporting in writing.
3. Take complete responsibility for the business and for each person you hire. Refuse to make excuses or blame others.
4. Act immediately when a problem arises—don't let it fester and grow. Every big problem was once a small problem and could have been solved easily at that time.
5. Keep a tight rein on employees. They are often like children and will try to get away with poor work and excuses.
6. When a person acts poorly or a deal starts to go sideways, take action immediately. Do not wish and hope that things will get better.
7. Document key disagreements in writing. Never trust to memory or to "he said, she said" recollections of conversations.
8. Have witnesses present for critical discussions, especially when disciplining or firing someone.
9. Check references and backgrounds of job applicants thoroughly. More than 50% of them are inaccurate or false.
10. Address problems and issues directly and immediately. Deal face to face and don't be afraid to confront a difficult person or situation.
11. Hire slow and fire fast. Take your time in making a hiring decision. If you realize that you've made a mistake, cut your losses quickly and let the person go.
12. Be careful about throwing gasoline on the fire. Don't say or write anything when you are angry.

13. If litigation arises as a possibility, get a good lawyer and walk through each step of the case, just like a real estate closing—right away.
14. Keep your ego and emotions out of it as long and as much as possible; rise above it. Resolve to remain calm.
15. Work only with people whom you like, trust, enjoy, and respect, and with whom you feel open and comfortable. Refuse to work with difficult, negative, or stressful people.
16. Put a "binding arbitration" clause in every contract.
17. Settle early and cheap whenever possible.
18. Meet and discuss to find a non-legal, non-litigious solution early.
19. Be meticulous, correct, and fully documented.
20. Write every contract and agreement as if it were to become the basis of a lawsuit.
21. Pay more for good legal advice in advance.
22. Organize all your personal finances so they are untouchable in a lawsuit.
23. Build legal firewalls for trusts, family limited partnerships, LLCs, etc.
24. Expect to be sued in the course of business and be thoroughly prepared, emotionally and financially.

There is no place where "an ounce of protections is worth a pound of cure" than in protecting yourself from lawsuits and claims.

CHAPTER SIX

Personal Blueprints

In this chapter:

1.	The Seven Mental Laws of Success	204
2.	Personal Analysis	207
3.	Seven Qualities of Self-Made Millionaires	216
4.	Personal Effectiveness Assessment	217
5.	List of Values	219
6.	Achieving Clarity with Your Goals	221
7.	Seven Questions for Goal Setting	223
8.	Major Definite Purpose	225
9.	Seven Key Concepts for Success	226
10.	Seven Truths About You	229

Way to Wealth Workbook: Blueprints for Business Success

1. Seven Mental Laws of Success

Fully 80% of everything you accomplish will be mental. It will be determined by the way you think and feel. For more than 5,000 years, different mental laws and principles have been discovered and taught, right up to the present day. Here are the most important:

1. **The Law of Control:** You feel positive about yourself to the degree that you feel in control of your own life. In what areas do you feel most in control?

    1. _____
    2. _____
    3. _____

    This law says that you experience the greatest unhappiness and stress to the degree that you feel that part of your life is controlled by other people or circumstances. In what areas do you feel controlled by others?

2. **The Law of Cause and Effect:** There is a cause for every effect. Everything happens for a reason. If there is something in your life you want, you must do what other successful people have done to get what they have wanted. What three things could you do immediately to help you to achieve one of your goals?

    1. _____
    2. _____
    3. _____

    If there is something in your life that you don't want, what are its causes and what could you do to remove them?

3. **The Law of Belief:** Whatever you believe, with feeling or conviction, becomes your reality, whether the belief is true or false. What beliefs do you hold deeply about yourself and life?

    1. _____
    2. _____
    3. _____

Chapter 6. Personal Blueprints

What are some of your self-limiting beliefs that might be holding you back?

1. _____
2. _____
3. _____

4. **The Law of Expectations:** Whatever you expect, with confidence, becomes a self-fulfilling prophecy for you. What do you confidently expect is going to happen to and for you?

    1. _____
    2. _____
    3. _____

5. **The Law of Attraction:** You are a "living magnet" and you invariably attract into your life the people, ideas, and situations that are in harmony with your dominant thoughts and emotions. What people and situations have you attracted into your life with your current thinking?

    1. _____
    2. _____
    3. _____

6. **The Law of Concentration:** Whatever you concentrate on grows and increases in your life. What do you think about most of the time?

    1. _____
    2. _____
    3. _____

7. **The Law of Correspondence:** Your outer life corresponds to your inner life; your world is a mirror of what is going on inside of you. If you want to change something on the outside, you must change something you are thinking on the inside. In what three areas of your life do your outer events correspond with your innermost thoughts?

   1. _____

   2. _____

   3. _____

Notes

Chapter 6. Personal Blueprints

2. Personal Analysis

The better you know and understand yourself, the better decisions you can make and the better results you will get. Answer the following questions:

1. What is your current **position**? _____

2. What are the **three most important things** you do in your work?

    1. _____
    2. _____
    3. _____

3. How do you **measure results, success, and accomplishments** in your work?

    1. _____
    2. _____
    3. _____

4. What are your **special abilities and talents**?

    1. _____
    2. _____
    3. _____

5. What tasks do you **perform especially well**?

    1. _____
    2. _____
    3. _____

6. What are your **three most important goals** in your work?

    1. _____
    2. _____
    3. _____

Way to Wealth Workbook: Blueprints for Business Success

What **specific actions** could you take immediately to achieve these goals?

1. _____
2. _____
3. _____

7. What are your **three most important goals** in your family and personal life?

   1. _____
   2. _____
   3. _____

   What **specific actions** could you take immediately to achieve these goals?

   1. _____
   2. _____
   3. _____

8. What are your three most important **financial goals**?

   1. _____
   2. _____
   3. _____

   What **specific actions** could you take immediately to achieve these goals?

   1. _____
   2. _____
   3. _____

9. What are your three most important **health goals**?

   1. _____
   2. _____
   3. _____

Chapter 6. Personal Blueprints

What **specific actions** could you take immediately to achieve these goals?

1. _____
2. _____
3. _____

10. What are your three most important **career goals**?

    1. _____
    2. _____
    3. _____

    What **specific actions** could you take immediately to achieve these goals?

    1. _____
    2. _____
    3. _____

11. What **three skills** could you develop that would help you the most to achieve your most important goals?

    1. _____
    2. _____
    3. _____

    What **specific actions** could you take immediately to achieve these goals?

    1. _____
    2. _____
    3. _____

12. What are the **three greatest opportunities** in your life right now?

    1. _____
    2. _____
    3. _____

Way to Wealth Workbook: Blueprints for Business Success

What could you do immediately to **take advantage** of these opportunities?

1. _____
2. _____
3. _____

13. What are your **three biggest worries** or concerns in life right now?

    1. _____
    2. _____
    3. _____

    What steps could you take immediately to **resolve these worries** or concerns?

    1. _____
    2. _____
    3. _____

14. What **three qualities** do you have that you are most proud of?

    1. _____
    2. _____
    3. _____

15. What **three weaknesses** do you have that you would like to overcome?

    1. _____
    2. _____
    3. _____

16. What **three words** would you like people to use to describe you when you die?

    1. _____
    2. _____
    3. _____

Chapter 6. Personal Blueprints

17. What are your **three most important business values**?

    1. _____
    2. _____
    3. _____

18. What are the three most **important values** that guide your **relationships** with your family and others?

    1. _____
    2. _____
    3. _____

19. Who are the **most important people** in your work?

Name	**Position**
1. _____	_____
2. _____	_____
3. _____	_____
4. _____	_____
5. _____	_____
6. _____	_____
7. _____	_____

20. Who are the most important people in **your personal life**?

Name	**Relationship**
1. _____	_____
2. _____	_____
3. _____	_____
4. _____	_____
5. _____	_____

Way to Wealth Workbook: Blueprints for Business Success

      Name   **Relationship**

    6. _____   _____

    7. _____   _____

21. What are your favorite **non-work activities**?

    1. _____

    2. _____

    3. _____

22. What would you do if you were forced to **take a day off**?

    1. _____

    2. _____

    3. _____

23. What would you do if you were forced to **take a month off** and you had an unlimited budget?

    1. _____

    2. _____

    3. _____

24. What would you do with your life if you learned today that you only had **six months to live**?

    1. _____

    2. _____

    3. _____

25. What would you do with your time if you had $20 milliom in the bank but only **ten years to live**?

    1. _____

    2. _____

    3. _____

Chapter 6. Personal Blueprints

26. What goals would you set for yourself if you were **guaranteed** complete success?

    1. _____

    2. _____

    3. _____

27. What **three activities in your life** or your work make you happiest and give you the greatest feeling of self-esteem?

    1. _____

    2. _____

    3. _____

28. What three activities or tasks do you **enjoy the least**?

    1. _____

    2. _____

    3. _____

29. If you could do only **one thing all day long** at work, what one activity contributes the most value to your company?

    1. _____

    2. _____

    3. _____

30. What are the **three most valuable things** you do in your work?

    1. _____

    2. _____

    3. _____

31. If you could wave a **magic wand** and make your life perfect in every respect, what would your life look like?

   1. Work and Career? _____

   2. Family and Relationships? _____

   3. Financial Situation? _____

   4. Health and Fitness? _____

   5. Personal or Social Life? _____

32. **Knowing what you now know**, is there any situation you would not get into today if you had to do it over?

   1. Work? _____

   2. Employees? _____

   3. Investments? _____

   4. Health? _____

   5. Family? _____

   6. People? _____

   7. Choices? _____

   8. Other? _____

33. List your **ten most important goals** in life right now. Start each goal with "I." Write in the present, positive tense, as though it were already a reality.

   1. _____

   2. _____

   3. _____

   4. _____

   5. _____

   6. _____

   7. _____

   8. _____

Chapter 6. Personal Blueprints

9. _____

10. _____

34. Imagine that you could achieve one of the above goals **within 24 hours**. Which **one goal** would have the greatest positive impact on your life?

_____

_____

Notes

3. Seven Qualities of Self-Made Millionaires

Thousands of self-made millionaires have been interviewed and studied over the years to find out how and why they are different from the average person. It seems that self-made millionaires have certain qualities of character developed to a higher level than most people.

Give yourself a grade of 1–10 on each of these qualities:

1. **Focused:** They spend **10–20 hours each month studying**, thinking about saving and investments. _____

2. **Long-term oriented:** They set financial goals 10 and 20 years out—and stick to them. _____

3. **Frugal:** They are careful with their money. _____

4. **Self-disciplined:** They practice self-restraint, refusing to take the line of least resistance and to seek immediate gratification. _____

5. **Courageous:** they are willing to take intelligent risks toward their goals. _____

6. **Hard-working:** They average 59 hours per week. _____

7. **Persistent:** They never give up—ever. _____

Notes

Chapter 6. Personal Blueprints

4. Personal Effectiveness Assessment

The starting point of becoming more effective is for you to analyze yourself to determine your strengths and weaknesses, and determine where you can improve. Sometimes, the development or strengthening of a single quality can change the course of your life.

1. What are your most important **values**? What do you stand for, believe in, care about the most? (See the list of possible values, next section.)

    1. _____   4. _____

    2. _____   5. _____

    3. _____   6. _____

2. What are your **main goals** in the four main areas of your life?

    1. Financial? _____

    2. Business? _____

    3. Family? _____

    4. Health? _____

3. On a scale of 1–10, how often do you **plan each day**, set priorities, and concentrate on the most valuable use of your time?

    1. Daily planning? _____

    2. Clear priorities? _____

    3. Focus and concentrate? _____

4. On a scale of 1–10, how well do you take excellent care of your **physical health**?

    1. Proper diet? _____

    2. Proper exercise? _____

    3. Proper rest? _____

    4. Proper weight? _____

    5. Overall level of health and fitness? _____

5. On a scale of 1–10, how well do you balance your time satisfactorily among **work, family, and personal activities**?

    1. Between work and family? _____

    2. Between family and personal activities? _____

    3. Between personal activities and work? _____

6. On a scale of 1–10, how consistently do you continue to **learn, grow, and improve** each day?

    1. Books: how many minutes or hours do you read each day? _____

    2. How many magazines do you read each month? _____

    3. How many hours of audio programs do you listen to in your car or exercising each day, week, month? _____

    4. How many seminars do you attend each year? _____

    5. How many educational courses do you take each year, through traditional or online colleges? _____

7. On a scale of 1–10, how well do you feel that you are making **steady progress** toward achieving your ideal goals in the following areas?

    1. Business, career, and income? _____

    2. Family, relationships, and lifestyle? _____

    3. Financial independence? _____

    4. Excellent health and fitness? _____

What **one action** should you take immediately based on your answers to these questions?

_____

_____

Chapter 6. Personal Blueprints

5. List of Values

Accuracy	Energy	Joyfulness
Adaptability	Enjoyment	Kindness
Adventure	Enterprise	Knowledge
Affection	Enthusiasm	Leadership
Alertness	Excellence	Learning
Ambition	Faith	Love
Assertiveness	Flexibility	Loyalty
Authenticity	Focus	Maturity
Beauty	Forgiveness	Method
Boldness	Freedom	Meticulousness
Broad-mindedness	Friendliness	Modesty
Calmness	Fulfillment	Naturalness
Capability	Generosity	Nurture
Care	Gentleness	Optimism
Career	Good attitude	Organization
Clear-thinking	Good balance	Originality
Compassion	Good humor	Patience
Competence	Growth	Peace
Confidence	Happiness	Perseverance
Conscientiousness	Health	Persistence
Consideration	Helpfulness	Playfulness
Contribution	Honesty	Pleasantness
Cooperation	Hope	Politeness
Courage	Humility	Possessiveness
Creativity	Imagination	Practicality
Dependability	Impartiality	Precision
Determination	Independence	Professionalism
Diligence	Innovation	Progress
Dynamism	Integrity	Prosperity
Education	Intelligence	Punctuality
Effectiveness	Joviality	Purposefulness

Quality	Strength	Value
Quickness	Tact	Versatility
Resourcefulness	Talent	Victory
Respect	Teamwork	Vigor
Responsibility	Thankfulness	Warmth
Self-control	Thoroughness	Willpower
Sensibility	Tolerance	Wisdom
Sincerity	Trustworthiness	Wit
Sociability	Understanding	Youthfulness
Specialness	Uniqueness	Zeal

Notes

Chapter 6. Personal Blueprints

6. Achieving Clarity with Your Goals

The greater clarity you have regarding your business and financial goals, the more rapidly you will achieve them.

1. What are your three most important **business or financial** goals right now?

    1. _____

    2. _____

    3. _____

2. How will you **measure success** in each area?

    1. _____

    2. _____

    3. _____

3. What are your **deadlines** for achieving each of these goals?

    1. _____

    2. _____

    3. _____

4. What three **actions** could you take immediately to help you achieve these goals?

    1. _____

    2. _____

    3. _____

5. What are the three **most valuable benefits** to you of achieving these goals?

    1. _____

    2. _____

    3. _____

6. What additional **resources, skills, people,** or **information** do you need to achieve these goals?

   1. _____

   2. _____

   3. _____

7. What **one result**, if you could achieve it, would help you the most to achieve these goals?

   1. _____

   2. _____

   3. _____

8. What **one step** are you going to take immediately to achieve these goals?

   1. _____

   2. _____

   3. _____

Notes

_____
_____
_____
_____
_____
_____
_____

Chapter 6. Personal Blueprints

7. Seven Questions for Goal Setting

1. What are your **values**? What are your most important virtues or organizing principles?

    1. _____
    2. _____
    3. _____
    4. _____
    5. _____

2. What are your **three most important** goals right now?

    1. _____
    2. _____
    3. _____

3. What would you do, how would you change your life, if you won **$1 million** cash, tax-free, today?

    1. _____
    2. _____
    3. _____

4. What would you do, how would you spend your time, if you learned today that you had only **six months to live**?

    1. _____
    2. _____
    3. _____

5. What have you always wanted to do but been **afraid to attempt**?

    1. _____
    2. _____
    3. _____

6. What sorts of activities, past or present, give you your **greatest feeling of importance**, of self-esteem?

   1. _____

   2. _____

   3. _____

7. What **one great thing** would you dare to dream if you knew you could not fail?
   _____
   _____

Notes

Chapter 6. Personal Blueprints

8. Major Definite Purpose

Whichever goal you selected as your **most important** goal in life today, write it out in detail:

1. Define your goal *clearly* **in writing**. Make it measurable. Be specific.

   _____

   _____

2. What is your **deadline** for achieving this goal? _____

3. What **obstacles** do you have to overcome, what problems do you have to solve, to achieve this goal?

   1. _____
   2. _____
   3. _____

4. What additional **knowledge, skills, and abilities** do you have to acquire or develop to achieve your goal?

   1. _____
   2. _____
   3. _____

5. Whose **cooperation, assistance, and support** do you require to achieve your goal?

   1. _____
   2. _____
   3. _____

6. What **steps** do you have to take to achieve this goal?

   1. _____
   2. _____
   3. _____

7. What *one step* will you take **immediately**?

   _____

WAY TO WEALTH WORKBOOK: BLUEPRINTS FOR BUSINESS SUCCESS

9. Seven Key Concepts for Success

Top people think and act better than average people. This is because they look at life with greater depth and introspection. Here are some of the best thinking tools ever discovered to help you to be more efficient and effective.

1. **Winning Edge Concept:** Small differences in ability often lead to large differences in results. List three areas in which, if you were excellent, you could greatly improve your performance and results.

    1. _____
    2. _____
    3. _____

2. **Key Result Areas:** There are generally only five to seven key result areas in each job. By continually improving in these areas, the cumulative effect on your overall results can be extraordinary. What are the key result areas of your work?

    1. _____
    2. _____
    3. _____
    4. _____
    5. _____
    6. _____
    7. _____

    What is your weakest area? What could you do immediately to begin to improve in this area?

    _____
    _____

Chapter 6. Personal Blueprints

3. **Critical Success Factors:** There are certain numbers, measures, or metrics that determine the health of your business and the result you are achieving in each area. What are yours?

   1. _____
   2. _____
   3. _____
   4. _____
   5. _____

4. **Long-Term Perspective:** The most successful people have a clear vision of what they want to accomplish and where they want to be in the future. If your life were perfect three to five years from now, what would it look like?

   1. Your business? _____
   2. Your income? _____
   3. Your family life? _____
   4. Your financial situation? _____
   5. Your health? _____

5. **Idealization:** Imagine that you could design your perfect calendar, week by week and month by month. If you were financially independent, how would you organize your life?

   1. _____
   2. _____
   3. _____
   4. _____
   5. _____

Way to Wealth Workbook: Blueprints for Business Success

6. **Area of Excellence:** You will fulfill your business and income potential only when you become excellent at the most important parts of your work. What are the three most important things you do, those activities that account for 90% or more of your contribution? On a scale of 1- 10, how good are you in each area?

Work Activity	Score
1. _____	_____
2. _____	_____
3. _____	_____

   What **one skill**, if you were excellent at it, would help you the most in your work and business?

   _____

   _____

   What could you do, starting immediately, to begin **improving** in that area?

   _____

   _____

7. **Completion and Closure:** All success requires the completion of key tasks and closure in key areas of your life. This requires self-discipline, persistence, and courage. What are three tasks or activities that you should complete immediately?

   1. _____

   2. _____

   3. _____

   In which three areas of your personal or business life do you need to bring about closure so that you can focus on your future?

   1. _____

   2. _____

   3. _____

Keep thinking about how you could improve in each of these areas.

Chapter 6. Personal Blueprints

10. Seven Truths About You

Each person has a certain amount of emotional baggage that goes back to early childhood and later experiences. As a result, people often feel inferior to others, no matter how successful they are. They doubt themselves and their abilities, and sometimes feel like imposters when they achieve greatly.

Perhaps the worst feeling is that of "inadequacy," or the feeling that "I'm not good enough." Until you get over these feelings, you continue to work hard on the outside but feel dissatisfied on the inside.

Here are seven truths that you must accept about yourself:

1. You are a thoroughly **good and excellent person**, valuable and worthy beyond measure. What are your three most admirable qualities?

    1. _____
    2. _____
    3. _____

2. **You are important**—to yourself and to many others whom you affect in some way. List three areas in which your time and activities are important.

    1. _____
    2. _____
    3. _____

3. You have **unlimited potential**, the ability to create your life and world as you desire. What three goals would you want to achieve if you had no limitations?

    1. _____
    2. _____
    3. _____

4. You **create your world** in every respect by the way you think and the depth of your conviction. What are your three deepest beliefs about yourself and your future?

    1. _____
    2. _____
    3. _____

5. You are always **free to choose** the content of your thoughts and the direction of your life. What do you think about most of the time?

   1. _____

   2. _____

   3. _____

6. You are put on this earth with a great destiny; you are meant to do **something wonderful** with your life. What would you want to do or accomplish for yourself or others if you had no limitations?

   1. _____

   2. _____

   3. _____

7. **There are no limits** to what you can do, be, or have except for the limits you place on your own thinking and your own imagination. What three self-limiting beliefs or excuses might be holding you back?

   1. _____

   2. _____

   3. _____

Doubt and fear are, and have always been, the worst enemies of mankind. Your life advances and improves as you free yourself from both of them.

Notes

_____

_____

_____

_____

_____

_____

CHAPTER SEVEN
Productivity and Performance Blueprints

In this chapter:

1. Seven Disciplines for Success — 232
2. Seven Steps to Better Time Management — 233
3. Seven Steps to Productivity Improvement — 234
4. Highest-Value Activities — 235
5. Seven Secrets of Superb Health — 238
6. The 1000% Formula — 240
7. Seven Steps to Mental Fitness — 242
8. Seven Keys to Achieving Balance in Life — 243
9. The Seven C's of Effectiveness — 245
10. Double Your Time Off — 247
11. Simplification — 249
12. Simplification Exercise — 250
13. Decision Making — 252
14. Seven Rules for the 21st Century — 253
15. Daily Affirmations — 254

1. Seven Disciplines for Success

Successful people are those who have successful habits. Good habits are hard to form, but easy to live with. They require hard work initially, but then become automatic and easy.

The habits or disciplines that lead to success are all learnable via repetition and practice.

1. **Daily goal-setting:** Develop the habit of writing out your ten most important goals each morning.
2. **Daily planning and organizing:** Develop the habit of planning each day in advance by making a list of everything you have to do.
3. **Daily priority setting:** Develop the habit of setting priorities on your list of activities before you begin.
4. **Daily concentration on highest-value activities:** Develop the habit of single-minded concentration on your most important task.
5. **Daily exercise and proper nutrition:** Develop the habit of exercising 30 or more minutes each day, preferably in the morning, right after you get up.
6. **Daily learning:** Reading, audio programs, courses. Develop the habit of continuous personal and professional improvement.
7. **Daily time for relationships:** Develop the habit of spending time with the most important people in your life each day.

When you develop these habits and practice these disciplines daily, you will achieve five and ten times the results of the average person.

Notes

Chapter 7. Productivity and Performance Blueprints

2. Seven Steps to Better Time Management

1. **Make a list** of everything you have to do each day, preferably the night before.
2. **Use the 80/20 Rule.** Identify the 20% of activities that account for 80% of the value of what you do.
3. **Use the ABCDE method** of setting priorities on your tasks.

   "A" tasks: must do—serious consequences if you do not do them

   "B" tasks: should do—only mild consequences if you do not do them

   "C" tasks: nice to do—no consequences whether you do them or not

   "D" tasks: delegate to anyone else who can do them, to free up more time for your "A" tasks

   "E" tasks—eliminate or discontinue whenever possible
4. **Use zero-based thinking.** Is there anything that you are doing today that you wouldn't start up again today, knowing what you know now?

   If the answer is "yes," one of the best time savers is to stop doing it.
5. **Practice the Law of Forced Efficiency:** There is never enough time to do everything, but there is always enough time to do the most important thing:
   1. What are your highest-value activities?
   2. Why are you on the payroll, specifically?
   3. What can you, and only you, do that will make a real difference, if you do it well?
6. **Overcome procrastination.** Whenever you feel like slowing down or stopping work on a key task, repeat the words, "Do it now!" over and over to impel you back to work.
7. **Concentrate single-mindedly** on one thing at a time. Select your most important task and dedicate yourself 100% to completing it, without diversion or distraction.

When you develop the habits of working on these behaviors every day, your productivity, performance and output will double and triple.

3. Seven Steps to Productivity Improvement

There are seven simple ways to double and triple your productivity, performance, and output each day:

1. **Work longer and harder.** Start one hour earlier, work through lunch and stay one hour later. This will add three hours to your day and increase your productivity by at least 50%.
2. **Work faster.** Pick up the pace. Resolve to move quickly throughout the day, as if you were under a tight deadline for a major task.
3. **Work on higher-value activities.** Concentrate on those tasks that are worth more than anything else.
4. **Work together.** Synergy and teamwork. Work with others to complete multitask jobs.
5. **Do things you're better at.** Focus on those tasks that you do quickly and easily, but that take others a lot of time.
6. **Bunch your tasks.** Do several similar tasks all together. This makes you more efficent and enables you to get more things done faster;
7. **Simplify, consolidate, eliminate low-value activities.** Stop doing things of low value so that you have more time for tasks of higher value.

The most important quality for success is self discipline, every single day, on these seven behaviors.

Notes
_____
_____
_____
_____
_____
_____
_____
_____
_____

Chapter 7. Productivity and Performance Blueprints

4. Highest-Value Activities

There are always certain activities that are **more valuable** than others, in every area.

Great success comes from identifying those activities and spending more time on them.

1. What are your highest-value activities in your **work**?

    1. _____
    2. _____
    3. _____

2. What are your highest-value activities in your **sales and marketing**?

    1. _____
    2. _____
    3. _____

3. What are your highest-value **administrative or support** activities in your work?

    1. _____
    2. _____
    3. _____

4. What are your highest-value **skills, talents, and abilities**?

    1. _____
    2. _____
    3. _____

5. What are the most important things you do in terms of achieving **financial independence**?

    1. _____
    2. _____
    3. _____

6. What are your highest-value activities with your **family**?

   1. _____

   2. _____

   3. _____

7. What are your highest-value activities in terms of your **health and fitness**?

   1. _____

   2. _____

   3. _____

8. What are the **highest-value skills** that you could learn or develop?

   1. _____

   2. _____

   3. _____

9. What are the **highest-value subjects** that you could learn about?

   1. _____

   2. _____

   3. _____

10. What are the most valuable contributions you could make to your **community and social activities**?

    1. _____

    2. _____

    3. _____

11. What are the most valuable things you can do to ensure a higher quality of **personal life**?

    1. _____

    2. _____

    3. _____

Chapter 7. Productivity and Performance Blueprints

12. What are you going to **do immediately** as a result of your answers to the above questions?

    1. _____

    2. _____

    3. _____

What one thing are you going to do first?

_____

_____

Notes
_____
_____
_____
_____
_____
_____
_____
_____
_____
_____
_____
_____
_____
_____
_____

5. Seven Secrets of Superb Health

There are seven things you can do to enjoy better health and more energy, based on 20 years of research on 8,000 adults.

1. **Proper weight:** Slightly under your the weight for your height and body type is best. What are three things you can do to ensure that you reach and stay at your proper weight?

    1. _____
    2. _____
    3. _____

2. **Proper diet:** Eat a wide variety of foods, choose lean source protein, and drink lots of water. What are three improvements you could make in your diet?

    1. _____
    2. _____
    3. _____

3. **Proper exercise:** Three to five times per week, for 200 minutes or more total. What are three activities you could do to get 200 minutes of exercise each week?

    1. _____
    2. _____
    3. _____

4. **Proper rest and relaxation:** You need seven to eight hours of sleep each night, one day off per week, and mini-vacations every two to three months. What steps could you take immediately to be better rested?

    1. _____
    2. _____
    3. _____

Chapter 7. Productivity and Performance Blueprints

5. **Proper nutritional and dietary supplements:** What vitamins, minerals, or nutrients should you add to your diet?

    1. _____
    2. _____
    3. _____

6. **No smoking:** This factor is the most important. Smoking is now associated with 32 illnesses and medical conditions.

    1. _____
    2. _____
    3. _____

7. **Moderate to nil alcohol consumption:** Everything in moderation!

    1. _____
    2. _____
    3. _____

Resolve today that you are going to live to be a hundred! Begin immediately to engage in the health habits that will get you there.

Notes

_____
_____
_____
_____
_____
_____

6. The 1000% Formula

Increase your income 1000%! By applying the Law of Incremental Improvement to your life, you can increase your productivity, performance, and output by 1000% in the years ahead.

Resolve to increase your productivity by 0.1% each day, five days per week. This amounts to 0.5% in five days. If you improve 0.5% for four weeks, you will be 2% more productive. If you continue for one year, 52 weeks, you will be 26% more productive. If you continue getting better at the rate of 0.1% per day, 0.5% percent each week, 26% each year, then in 10 years, with compounding, you will be producing and earning 1004% more than today.

Here are the seven steps to follow each day:

1. **Arise early and read one hour each day in your field.** This will translate into one book per week, 50 books per year, 500 books in 10 years, making you one of the best educated and skilled people in your field.

2. **Rewrite and review your major goals each morning.** Take a few minutes to rewrite them in a spiral notebook, programming them deeper into you subconscious mind.

3. **Plan every day in advance.** Make a list, set priorities, and be thoroughly organized before you start work.

4. **Always concentrate** on the most valuable use of your time, every minute of every day.

5. **Listen to educational audio programs in your car.** The average driver sits behind the wheel 500-1,000 hours each year. This is the equivalent of 12 to 24 40-hour weeks, three to six months, or the equivalent of attending a university full time. Audio listening and learning alone can give you a 1000% increase in income.

6. **Ask two questions** after every experience:
   1. What did I do right? Review your performance and think about all the good things you did.
   2. What would I do differently? Think of how you could improve your performance next time.

   When you ask and answer these questions, you focus on the best parts of your present and future performance and learn the most you can from everything you do.

Chapter 7. Productivity and Performance Blueprints

7. **Treat everyone you meet like a million-dollar customer.** When you treat others as if they are really important, you satisfy one of the deepest of all subconscious needs. This simple rule is the key to excellent human relations, both in business and at home.

The law of incremental improvement and the law of accumulation, in combination, enable you to improve the quality of your life and increase your income substantially in the years ahead.

Notes

7. Seven Steps to Mental Fitness

Mental fitness is like physical fitness. You develop it with training and practice. Here are the seven keys to becoming a completely positive person:

1. **Positive self-talk:** Use affirmations—positive, present tense, and personal: "I like myself!" "I can do it!" "I feel terrific!"

2. **Positive visualization:** See your goals as already achieved. Create a clear, exciting picture of your goal and replay this picture in your mind.

3. **Positive people:** Associate with winners. Avoid negative people. Resolve not to have stressful people in your life.

4. **Positive mental food:** Feed your mind with positive reading, listening, and viewing.

5. **Positive training and development:** Dedicate yourself to lifelong learning and personal improvement.

6. **Positive health habits:** Eat well, exercise regularly, and get sufficient rest and relaxation.

7. **Positive expectations:** Look for the good in every person and situation.

Notes

_____
_____
_____
_____
_____
_____
_____
_____

Chapter 7. Productivity and Performance Blueprints

8. Seven Keys to Achieving Balance in Life

Your ability to balance your work and personal life is essential to your happiness and well-being. Here are seven things you must do:

1. **Set peace of mind as your highest goal.** What are three activities or pastimes that give you the greatest sense of inner peace?

    1. _____
    2. _____
    3. _____

2. **Make your happiness your chief aim in life.** What three activities make you the happiest?

    1. _____
    2. _____
    3. _____

3. Put your **relationships** ahead of all else. Who are the most important people in your life?

    1. _____
    2. _____
    3. _____

4. Define your **ideal lifestyle** and commit to create it. What three parts of your life or work do you enjoy the most?

    1. _____
    2. _____
    3. _____

Way to Wealth Workbook: Blueprints for Business Success

5. When you work, **work all the time you work**. What are the three most important things you do in your work?

   1. _____

   2. _____

   3. _____

6. When you're with your **family**, be there 100% of the time. What three activities do you enjoy most with your family?

   1. _____

   2. _____

   3. _____

7. Create unbroken **chunks of time** with the most important people in your life. In what areas do you, or should you, spend more time with the members of your family?

   1. _____

   2. _____

   3. _____

Notes

_____
_____
_____
_____
_____
_____
_____

Chapter 7. Productivity and Performance Blueprints

9. The Seven C's of Effectiveness

There are seven areas of life where an improvement can lead to a dramatic increase in results.

1. **Clarity:** Know exactly what you want in every area of your life. What are your three most important goals in the following areas?

    1. Business and career?_____

    2. Family and relationships?_____

    3. Health and fitness? _____

    4. Money and finances? _____

2. **Competence:** Become extremely good at the key skills in your career. What are the three skills in which it is most important that you excel?

    1. _____

    2. _____

    3. _____

3. **Constraints:** Identify the factors that set the speed at which you achieve your goals. What is holding you back?

Goal	**Limiting Factor**
1. _____	_____
2. _____	_____
3. _____	_____

4. **Creativity:** Focus all your intelligence on removing your biggest single roadblock. What are three things you could do to start achieving your goals faster?

    1. _____

    2. _____

    3. _____

5. **Concentration:** Focus your time and energy on completing your most important task. What are your three most important tasks or activities?

   1. _____

   2. _____

   3. _____

6. **Consideration:** Be aware of the people around you and how you can behave in the most positive and productive way. What three things can you do with others to build and maintain better relationships?

   1. _____

   2. _____

   3. _____

7. **Character:** Always live consistent with the very best that you know. Never compromise your integrity. What are the three qualities or virtues you most admire in yourself and others?

   1. _____

   2. _____

   3. _____

You have the potential to be, do and have more than ever before. When you work on yourself every day, you eventually fulfill your potential and become everything you are truly capable of becoming.

Chapter 7. Productivity and Performance Blueprints

10. Double Your Time Off

Make a decision today to spend more time with your family and on your personal life. Your goal is to work to live rather than live to work. Begin by deciding what you will do with your time off.

1. What three activities do you **enjoy** the most when you are not working?

    1. _____
    2. _____
    3. _____

2. What are your three most enjoyable **vacation** destinations?

    1. _____
    2. _____
    3. _____

3. If you were forced to take **a day off** from work, what three things would you do?

    1. _____
    2. _____
    3. _____

4. What **leisure activities** do you enjoy most with your family or friends?

    1. _____
    2. _____
    3. _____

5. How would you spend your time if you had only **six months** left to live?

    1. _____
    2. _____
    3. _____

Way to Wealth Workbook: Blueprints for Business Success

6. If you won **$10 million** tomorrow, what would you change about the way you use your time?

   1. _____

   2. _____

   3. _____

7. What **actions** are you going to take immediately to increase your time off?

   1. _____

   2. _____

   3. _____

   What **one leisure activity** are you going to plan right now?

   _____

   _____

Notes

Chapter 7. Productivity and Performance Blueprints

11. Simplification

There are several ways for you to simplify your life and simultaneously get more done.

1. **Delegate:** Develop the habit of delegating everything you can to people who work at a lower hourly rate than you.

2. **Outsource:** Assign every business or home task you can to other people or companies that specialize in that area.

3. **Eliminate:** The only way you can get control of your time is by stopping doing things that are no longer of any real value to you.

4. **Consolidate:** Do an entire job at once from start to finish, rather than starting and stopping several times.

5. **Downsize:** Reduce the number of your operations, products, services, and activities to the 20% that contribute most of the value.

6. **Delay, defer:** Put things off until later. Remember: "If it does not have to be done now, then it has to not be done now."

7. **Improve:** Continually get better at the most important things you do. This dramatically reduces the time required and simplifies your life.

Notes

12. Simplification Exercise

1. What three tasks could you **delegate** to someone else?

    1. _____
    2. _____
    3. _____

2. What three business activities could you **outsource** to others who could do them as well or better than you?

    1. _____
    2. _____
    3. _____

3. What three activities could you **eliminate** altogether?

    1. _____
    2. _____
    3. _____

4. What three tasks could you **consolidate** so that you or someone else could do them faster?

    1. _____
    2. _____
    3. _____

5. What three business activities could you **downsize** with no real loss?

    1. _____
    2. _____
    3. _____

Chapter 7. Productivity and Performance Blueprints

6. What three activities or projects could you **defer** or **delay** into the future to free up your time or the time of others?

    1. _____
    2. _____
    3. _____

7. In what three areas could you **improve** your skills and abilities so that you could do your most important work faster?

    1. _____
    2. _____
    3. _____

8. What **specific actions** are you going to take immediately as the result of your answers to the questions above?

    1. _____
    2. _____
    3. _____

You can only get your time under control to the degree to which you stop doing certain tasks. You must set "posteriorities" as well as priorities. Most of your results and rewards will come from a small number of activities.

WAY TO WEALTH WORKBOOK: BLUEPRINTS FOR BUSINESS SUCCESS

13. Decision Making

Action is everything! Take a few minutes to summarize your decisions from your answers to the questions above.

1. What one change are you going to make in your **work**?

   _____
   _____

2. What one change are you going to make in your **family life**?

   _____
   _____

3. What one change are you going to make in your **financial affairs**?

   _____
   _____

4. What one change are you going to make in your **health and fitness** activities?

   _____
   _____

5. What one subject are you going to **learn or improve** in?

   _____
   _____

6. What one activity are you going to do in your **social and community life**?

   _____
   _____

7. What one activity are you going to engage in to improve your **spiritual life**?

   _____
   _____

What **one action** are you going to take immediately?

_____
_____

Chapter 7. Productivity and Performance Blueprints

14. Seven Rules for the 21st Century

1. Your life gets better only when you get better.
2. It doesn't matter where you're coming from; all that matters is where you're going.
3. Anything worth doing well is worth doing poorly at first.
4. You are only as free as your options, the alternatives available to you.
5. Within every difficulty you face, there is the seed of an equal or greater advantage or benefit.
6. You can learn anything you need to learn to achieve any goal you can set for yourself.
7. The only real limits on what you can do or be are the limits you accept in your own mind.

Notes

15. Daily Affirmations

When you use positive affirmations, and talk to yourself positively all the time, you program your subconscious mind to help you to be a more efficient, effective, and happy person.

Fully 95% of your emotions are determined by the way you talk to yourself, and the way you interpret events to yourself, for good or ill. Resolve today to feed your mind with a steady stream of positive and uplifting messages until they become a permanent part of your attitude, behavior and personality.

Say these words to yourself over and over.

1. I get up and get going easily and immediately.
2. I read something educational, motivational, or spiritual for 30–60 minutes each morning.
3. I rewrite and review my top ten goals every morning.
4. I plan every day in advance by making a list of every task I intend to accomplish.
5. I set priorities on my task list before I begin working, using the ABCDE method.
6. I always begin work on my A-1 task.
7. I work single-mindedly on my most important task and I persist at it until it is 100% complete.
8. I am punctual and well prepared for every appointment and meeting.
9. I eat highly nutritious foods, drink lots of water, and avoid sugars, fats, and white-flour products.
10. I exercise for 30 minutes or more each day.
11. I take time to meditate or sit in solitude for 30 minutes each day.
12. I spend time with the most important people in my life each day and I treat them as if they were my best customers.

The more often you repeat these positive messages to yourself, the better you feel and the more effective and happy you become.

About the Author

Brian Tracy is one of America's top business speakers, a best-selling author, and one of the leading consultants and trainers on personal and professional development in the world today. He addresses 250,000 people each year on subjects ranging from personal success and leadership to managerial effectiveness, creativity, and sales.

He has written more than 45 books and has produced more than 350 audio and video learning programs. Brian's books have been translated into 36 languages and are being used in 52 countries. He is co-author, with Campbell Fraser, of the Advanced Coaching and Mentoring Program and the Coaching Excellence Program.

Brian has consulted with more than 1,000 companies—IBM, McDonnell Douglas, and The Million Dollar Round Table among them—and has trained more than 2,000,000 people. His ideas are proven, practical, and fast-acting. His readers, seminar participants, and coaching clients learn a series of techniques and strategies that they can use immediately to get better results in their lives and careers.

Brian Tracy University of Sales and Entrepreneurship

To earn more, you must learn more! Now you can learn practical proven strategies to attract more customers, make more sales, and increase your profits.

Brian Tracy University offers a complete series of practical, proven programs that have been applied successfully by more than 1,000,000 students in 46 countries, based on work with more than 1,000 companies.

There are four colleges of study for you to choose from:

1. **College of Sales and Sales Management.** This 30-part home study program shows you how to double and triple your sales, leads to a "Certified Sales Professional" designation.

2. **College of Entrepreneurship and Business Success.** Learn the tools and techniques you need to build a highly profitable, fast growth business, leads to a "Master of Business Excellence" certification.

3. **College of Management and Leadership.** In this 30-part "High Performance Leadership" program, you learn how to recruit, hire, manage, motivate, and build a top team of excellent people, leads to a "Master of Management" certificate.

4. **College of Personal Performance.** Learn how to set and achieve goals, set priorities, build your self-esteem and self-confidence, solve problems, and make better decisions, leading to a "Master of Personal Excellence" certification.

In one hour per week, with video, audio, CD, DVDs, books, and exercises, you can become one of the most skilled and highest paid people in your field. You learn how to increase your income and improve your profitability immediately.

Visit **Briantracyu.com** today and take a FREE assessment to discover your strengths and weaknesses and learn how to achieve personal excellence in everything you do.

Brian Tracy University
462 Stevens Avenue, Suite 202
Solana Beach, CA 92075
866-505-8345
Briantracyu.com

Business Coaching Opportunity

FocalPoint International Powered by Brian Tracy
Become a Certified Coach and Consultant!

Fully 20% of business owners have coaches today. *Fortune* magazine reports that coaches help companies make or save $10 to $15 for each dollar paid in coaching fees.

If you have business experience, and you like the idea of helping business owners improve their marketing, increase their sales, and boost their profits, FocalPoint Coaching could be the ideal business decision for you.

The business and coaching experts at FocalPoint will train you thoroughly in every part of the business coaching profession. You will learn how to conduct a complete business analysis, recommend improvements, and increase the profitability of your clients.

For more information on joining the *highest rated* Business Coaching Franchise in the United States, contact us:

Phone **877-433-6225**

e-mail us at **coaching@focalpointcoaching.com**

or visit our website at **www.focalpointcoaching.com**

Brian Tracy—Speaker, Author, Consultant

Brian Tracy is one of the top business and personal success speakers in the world today. He has given more than 5,000 talks and seminars for more than 1,000 companies, including many of the world's largest.

He gives fast-moving, entertaining, high-content speeches and seminars to 250,000 people each year, speaking in 46 countries on six continents.

His hard-hitting talks on *leadership, sales, management,* and *personal success* bring about immediate and long-lasting change. Many of his graduates have gone on to great success and fortune after a single talk.

Brian has written 45 books, and produced more than 350 audio and video learning programs. His books and courses have been translated into 36 languages and are used in 52 countries. He is the top audio author in the world today.

Brian is available for talks and seminars worldwide. He carefully crafts and tailors each talk for your unique audience, using your industry and examples throughout.

Talk and Seminar Subjects:

1. High Performance Selling

2. Leadership for the 21st Century

3. Performing at Your Best

4. Superior Sales Management

To book Brian to speak for your company or group please phone 858-481-2977 extension 17 or e-mail **VRisling@briantracy.com**.